Phil Munsey believes that everything about you matters—and his book, *Legacy Now*, is packed with principles for living with a legacy perspective. My own passion for training millions of leaders around the world through Equip is mirrored in the passion my friend Phil Munsey has for legacy. There is no true success without a successor, and training leaders and establishing legacy are cornerstones for insuring success for generations to come. Begin your legacy now—this book can be your guide.

—John C. Maxwell
Author, Speaker, and Founder,
INJOY Stewardship Services and EQUIP

Phil is not just an old friend with a distant relationship; he is a close friend who has proven his friendship. He is among the wisest counselors that speak into my life, as well as the lives of many other highly placed notable leaders. Content to be behind the scenes, it is time to make his revolutionary thinking public. When you read this book, you will understand why many seek him out for advice and direction. I personally don't know how I would cope without his voice speaking into my life. Phil Munsey knows how you can shape your legacy. Listen and learn from his incredible insights.

—Tommy Tenney
Author, *The God Chasers*
Godchasers Ministry

This remarkable book by my friend Phil Munsey is a must-read for the spiritual and secular person alike, because everyone leaves a legacy. Learn how your future self can create the present to feel the presence of heaven on earth. This is going to be a best seller for eternity!

—Harold H. Bloomfield, MD
New York Times Best-Selling Author of Nineteen Books

The first time I met Phil Munsey, the first words out of my mouth were, "There's a book in you." I am so delighted that book is no longer in Phil's heart but in your hands now. *Legacy Now* is God's solution to the agony of the human dilemma. May your heart be hungry to know the heavenly Spot Remover who takes our inferior interior and makes it superior!

—Mike Evans
#1 *New York Times* Best-Selling Author

Congratulations, Phil. Your book, *Legacy Now*, is a remarkable one, and it arrives at a time when it is most needed. Success in life is being sold as a gaudy, greedy collection of getting more money, more fame, and more power. When I'm asked what the most rewarding thing is in my life, I can proudly say it is my seventy-three-year marriage and the wonderful collection of thirty-six people in my family living happily and fulfilling my prayerful wishes. That's what *Legacy Now* is, and you have captured it in your book.

—ART LINKLETTER
TELEVISION PERSONALITY AND HOST

Phil Munsey has the unique ability to encourage and challenge, entertain and educate, make us laugh and cry—all at the same time! He is one of the most creative thinkers I know—often reexamining long-held notions and assumptions. Still, while many who think outside the box take us on futile detours into the bizarre in an attempt to come up with startling innovations, *Legacy Now* opens our eyes to the core matters of life. And, most importantly, this book shows how our individual lives really do matter.

—DR. JIM REEVE
SENIOR PASTOR, FAITH COMMUNITY CHURCH

I am honored to call Phil Munsey a friend. His life and ministry have advanced the kingdom of God in tremendous ways. Phil is the *real deal*. He lives what he writes, teaches, and preaches, just as Jesus did. I have read this book and recommend that you do as well.

—DR. WALT KALLESTAD
SENIOR PASTOR, COMMUNITY CHURCH OF JOY

When Phil Munsey speaks, I listen. His words of revelation and relevance stir my spirit and mind. You will come to understand the power, purpose, and the perpetuation of the blood of Jesus as you've never seen before. The "seed-to-deed" principle takes seed faith to another level. *Legacy Now* may be the most important book you read for a long time.

—DR. ORAL ROBERTS
FORMER CHANCELLOR, ORAL ROBERTS UNIVERSITY

I still remember the first time I heard Phil say, "Every deed produces a seed." It was a life lesson that as a father of five children I have never forgotten. *Legacy Now* is a profound book from one of the sharpest minds in the body of Christ. You'll learn how to perpetuate your faith to your children for generations to come.

—JENTEZEN FRANKLIN
SENIOR PASTOR, FREE CHAPEL

Legacy Now is a vibrant, eternity-echoing book that will cause your soul to awaken and grasp the eternal. My friend Phil Munsey has captured the heart and soul of what we should be as humanity—legacy builders. This book should be read by every person in every tribe, language, and tongue in order to have an effective life today and for all of eternity. *Legacy Now* communicates age-old biblical truth in the relevant vernacular of today's language to create a new generation of legacy builders! This is a must-read!

—JOHN BEVERE
AUTHOR/SPEAKER, COFOUNDER OF MESSENGER INTERNATIONAL

We have seen the reasons why we must have faith; we have heard why we need to release past hurts and issues in our lives; we have been taught that we are to remain true to God, our spouse, and our family because of the benefits these bring to us. But Phil Munsey helps us discover that these things leave imprints, not just on our own lives but also on the next generation, and the next, and the next. He beckons us to be heritage builders for our own family tree. When Phil shows us how much one very small deed can affect our seed, we find ourselves in the battle of lifetimes (not just one lifetime). He challenges us to believe that it is our turn to create a destiny for tomorrow's society. I dare you to read this book and discover a future that lies beyond yourself. When your great-great-grandchild looks up his or her family lineage, what do you want them to read about you? Phil's book will give you the foundation for your legacy.

—BISHOP HARRY R. JACKSON JR.
SENIOR PASTOR, HOPE CHRISTIAN CHURCH
CHAIRMAN, HIGH IMPACT LEADERSHIP COALITION

Phil Munsey is a brilliant pastor and a good friend to my family and to me. Growing up in a home of ministers, Phil realized the heritage he has and how he and Jeannie, as well as those who are parents, can pass it on to future generations. My five children and their spouses, who are all in the ministry, will forever tell the good news about the Lord Jesus Christ and about why everything about you matters to Him! What a legacy! I salute you, Phil. I'm proud of you.

—DODIE OSTEEN
COFOUNDER, LAKEWOOD CHURCH

When you read this book, *Legacy Now*, it will change your whole thinking process about how to view what you want in and from life. You will begin to figure out the answer to the secret of generational curses and generational blessings that will be revealed to your understanding in this book called *Legacy Now*. I'm proud to call this author "brother." What he has written will make a difference in thousands of lives, not only in this generation but also in generations to come.

—STEVE MUNSEY
SENIOR PASTOR, FAMILY CHRISTIAN CENTER

Everyone leaves a legacy; the question is, "Is it by design or default?" In this book, Phil Munsey helps you, the reader, to leave a strong legacy of faith for the next generation.

—KEVIN GERALD
SENIOR PASTOR, CHAMPIONS CENTRE

One of the most progressive thinkers and communicators I know of in the spiritual sector as well as in the marketplace is Phil Munsey. His ability to stimulate and provoke contemplation on powerful insights that produce prophetic momentum with its resultant motivational force is unmatched amongst his peers. Whether you are a parent, a Fortune 500 CEO, or a student, take your time and let this distinctive voice that is crying out in a twenty-first-century wilderness of distracting echoes lead you into the specific significance of your singular and shared destiny. Discover your legacy and the reason why everything about you really does matter.

—MARK J. CHIRONNA, MA, PhD
MARK CHIRONNA MINISTRIES
SENIOR PASTOR, THE MASTER'S TOUCH INTERNATIONAL CHURCH

Phil is one of our greatest friends in all the world. Full of passion and driven to reach the lost, he is a rare gift to the kingdom of God. Phil's new book takes the reader on a journey that truly teaches what it means to live a life totally dedicated unto God. The legacy concept is such a revolutionary way of understanding how our actions and thoughts affect the outcome of our lives. I have read this book and know that it will change people for the better. Once you pick it up, you will not be able to put it down.

—MATTHEW BARNETT
COFOUNDER OF DREAM CENTER LOS ANGELES

Phil Munsey is one of the wisest men I know, and his book, *Legacy Now*, will give you extraordinary insight into the meaning of a generational transfer—how our beliefs, actions, and decisions affect future generations. One important value for a kingdom leader to have is to leave a legacy, and this book tells us how to do it. I highly recommend it. I am certain it will change your life forever!

—GUILLERMO MALDONADO
SENIOR PASTOR, KING JESUS INTERNATIONAL MINISTRIES

In today's secular culture, branding has taken the place of religion. But in a world where people have lost faith in religion, they still desperately need to find meaning. Without a purpose, organizations can't function, culture can't survive, and people have no reason to live. Phil Munsey understands the importance of discovering meaning and leaving a legacy for the future. *Legacy Now* has captured the cry of this culture, and if you want to discover how to make Christianity relevant again, then this is the book to read.

—Phil Cooke, PhD
Author, *Branding Faith: Why Some Churches and Non-Profits Impact the Culture and Other's Don't*

Our crippling "living in the now" mentality has robbed us. Phil takes the high ground to glimpse our yesterday, today, and forever tied together. This will change your entire perspective!

—Lee Ezell
Speaker, Best-Selling Author

Phil Munsey and I serve on the board of a major national ministry. Phil stays on the cutting edge of today's world. As he expresses, the decisions you make today and everything about you will determine your future and legacy. Read *Legacy Now*.

—John H Moon Sr.
President, Moon Credit Corp.

In his new book, *Legacy Now: Why Everything About You Matters*, Phil Munsey exposes the fallacy of this Tinseltown thinking. Legacy will lead you into the joy of discovering that God has something up His sleeves in regards to your life and future—a plan that was set in motion before you arrived on this planet. With genuine vulnerability, Phil shows us we don't have to pretend to be better than we really are because God created us to "fit" in His master plan. Legacy will convince you that each person is a destiny—a planned, on-purpose being that God wanted to cast in His unfolding play. After reading this, you will no longer be able to think about life in terms of making up your own story. Instead, you will long to find your place in the story being told by God. You will see that Earth was never meant to be a world for the "survival of the fittest"—it is a world for the predestined. God has a purpose and a place for everything. In this view, success and fulfillment can no longer be based on personal aggrandizement or actualization but on obediently finding the position predestined for us by God. Brilliant stuff!

—Ed Gungor
Senior Pastor, People's Church
New York Times Best-Selling Author, *There's More to the Secret*

I have had the pleasure of knowing Phil Munsey for many years. My life has been forever changed by his creative teaching, encouragement, and continuous challenging. By living eternally minded, he always challenges me to live and leave a legacy in all that I do. We all leave a legacy, good or bad. This book will help you realize the significance of generational living for God's kingdom. Powerful!

—GREG ALBERTYN
FOUNDER, DIAMOND CAPITAL GROUP
SUPERCROSS WORLD CHAMPION

WOW! Phil Munsey's book, *Legacy Now*, explores perhaps the most profound question that any one of us can ever ask: "What is your legacy?" During the last twenty years, I have been privileged to speak in over three thousand public schools and see firsthand the legacy of divorce, abuse, abandonment, and rejection. Today, as a corporate coach and leadership strategist, I often speak in the world's largest business seminars on the subject of leadership. Legacy is an invitation to leadership! Leadership begins with awareness and begs each one of us to ask ourselves, "What am I doing today that will not only determine my own circumstances tomorrow but will also affect the destiny of humanity for generations to come?"

Legacy Now is a book that will help you live with a transcendent cause! It is a recognition that while your life is not about you, what you do will ultimately impact what life is about for everyone you come into contact with.

—KEITH A. CRAFT
CORPORATE COACH/LEADERSHIP STRATEGIST

I am so happy that thousands are now going to be exposed to the gift that is Phil Munsey! His faithful pursuit of the kind of divine wisdom that *Legacy Now* presents is destined to change the course of history for someone. If you read it, it will be yours. I wholeheartedly endorse the book because I know the man.

—MIKE HAYES
FOUNDER, COVENANT CHURCH

Blessed with a keen mind to articulate his cutting-edge thoughts both in speaking and writing, Phil Munsey will indeed capture every reader with this challenging, provoking book that will indeed leave us a "legacy" of its own. I have known Phil Munsey for many years, and I am always amazed at the delivery of each subject he teaches with both life experience and divine revelation. I am always inspired by his unique, God-given ability to communicate old ideas and ideals with fresh insight. This new book is a must-read for every person who wants to touch future generations while taking responsibility of everything they do and insure that their lives will be a blessing. Great job, Phil!

—DAVID T. DEMOLA
PASTOR, FAITH FELLOWSHIP MINISTRIES

Phil Munsey communicates in a powerful and effective way the need to realize the magnitude of our choices. Our choices affect not only us but also those who will be connected to our future for many generations to come. For those who have been born into families and circumstances that present extreme challenges, this book brings great news and provides keys to help you overcome and begin to establish a legacy that will live forever.

—NANCY ALCORN
FOUNDER, MERCY MINISTRIES

For the first time that I am aware of, someone has finally matched the DNA discovery of our generation to the power and purpose of the blood of Christ. Wow! Now more than ever we can contemplate and celebrate the meaning of why Christ died and shed His precious blood for our sins. Christ has truly provided "prewashed genes," as Phil so cleverly describes in his fascinating book, *Legacy Now: Why Everything About You Matters!* Learn how building a godly legacy may be the most important task you'll ever achieve.

—PAUL F. CROUCH
FOUNDER AND PRESIDENT, TRINITY BROADCASTING NETWORK

At last, someone who endorses the entire human lineage and not just a dissected section of it. I never knew my great-great-grandfather. He passed long before I arrived. Whether he was a successful man I do not know. In all my forty-four years I have never paused to thank God for him. Today, for the first time, I did. Thank you, Phil Munsey, for pouring your heart into writing *Legacy Now*. You have helped me realize that the cast of humanity is much bigger than just the few generations that are on stage at the moment.

—WES BEAVIS
MOTIVATIONAL SPEAKER AND ENTERTAINER
INTERNATIONAL BEST-SELLING AUTHOR

Pastor Phil's *Legacy Now* exemplifies the tongue and pen of a ready writer. He has a certain sound that resonates with revelation and unique articulation.

Abraham, the friend of God, knew that he could command the legacy of his household. Solomon discovered in the midst of his many vanities that eternity was written in the heart of man. Shakespeare mused about the world as a stage and all men playing their seven acts. Francis Schaeffer asked, "How then shall we live?" Men continue on a quest for their destiny about that which really matters.

Phil takes the specifics of our historical roots and makes them dynamic. He also imparts hope in the transformation that the gospel produces in us all. In his unique and inimitable way, Phil has gleaned, gathered, and garnered a treasure trove like a roving bumblebee, extracting and condensing nectar—the stuff of legacy. It has been my pleasure to call this man my friend for more than twenty years. And for more than twelve years I have gratefully called him my pastor.

—Moses Vegh
Ambassador, Hope to the Nations

The truth and treasure in this message, *Legacy Now*, is both urgent and vital for the health and welfare of the generations who follow. We should each construct a heritage that can be built upon and grown in unrestrictive ways. Phil Munsey powerfully inspires as well as practically identifies concepts so everyone can build legacy in their lives and world.

—Lisa Bevere
Best-Selling Author, *Fight Like a Girl*
and *Kissed the Girls and Made Them Cry*

Phil Munsey is, in my opinion, one of "God's generals." He has not only a heart for the lost but also compassion and love for youth. During a time in which my own son Kyle was struggling with his purpose and his own direction, Phil was able to reach him in a way that Kyle could understand and identify with. I believe this is a must-read book that will not only inspire and encourage the believer but will also reach out to those who are searching for the answer to life's big question: what am I here for?

—Don Colbert, MD
Author, *Toxic Relief* and *The Seven Pillars of Health*

Phil Munsey's words about legacy serve as a beacon in a world darkened by the constant search for instant gratification. When we realize that our lives matter not just for today but also for tomorrow and on into eternity, we are motivated to make each moment count. This book eloquently examines the unique dichotomy of calling and destiny, reaffirming important truths about our Creator's purposeful design.

—Don Piper
Speaker and *New York Times* Best-Selling Author of
90 Minutes in Heaven

LEGACY
NOW

LEGACY
NOW

PHIL MUNSEY

Charisma
HOUSE
A STRANG COMPANY

Most Strang Communications/Charisma House/Siloam/FrontLine/ Excel Books/Realms products are available at special quantity discounts for bulk purchase for sales promotions, premiums, fund-raising, and educational needs. For details, write Strang Communications/Charisma House/Siloam/ FrontLine/Excel Books/Realms, 600 Rinehart Road, Lake Mary, Florida 32746, or telephone (407) 333-0600.

Legacy Now by Phil Munsey
Published by Charisma House
A Strang Company
600 Rinehart Road
Lake Mary, Florida 32746
www.charismahouse.com

Unless otherwise noted, all Scripture quotations are from the New King James Version of the Bible. Copyright © 1979, 1980, 1982 by Thomas Nelson, Inc., publishers. Used by permission.

Scripture quotations marked AMP are from the Amplified Bible. Old Testament copyright © 1965, 1987 by the Zondervan Corporation. The Amplified New Testament copyright © 1954, 1958, 1987 by the Lockman Foundation. Used by permission.

Scripture quotations marked NASU are from the New American Standard Bible—Updated Edition, Copyright © 1960, 1962, 1963, 1968, 1971, 1972, 1973, 1975, 1977, 1995 by The Lockman Foundation. Used by permission. (www.Lockman.org)

Scripture quotations marked NIV are from the Holy Bible, New International Version of the Bible. Copyright © 1973, 1978, 1984, International Bible Society. Used by permission.

Scripture quotations marked NLT are from the Holy Bible, New Living Translation, copyright © 1996, 2004. Used by permission of Tyndale House Publishers, Inc., Wheaton, IL 60189. All rights reserved.

Scripture quotations marked The Message are from *The Message: The Bible in Contemporary English,* copyright © 1993, 1994, 1995, 1996, 2000, 2001, 2002. Used by permission of NavPress Publishing Group.

Cover Design: Marvin Eans
Executive Design Director: Bill Johnson

Library of Congress Cataloging-in-Publication Data

Munsey, Phil.
  Legacy Now / Phil Munsey.
      p. cm.
  ISBN 978-1-59979-259-0
  1. Christian life. 2. Influence (Psychology)--Religious aspects--Christianity.
  3. Intergenerational relations--Religious aspects--Christianity. I. Title.
  BV4501.3.M854 2008
  248.4--dc22

                                              2007035726

First Edition

08 09 10 11 12 — 9 8 7 6 5 4 3 2 1
Printed in the United States of America

Legacy Now:
Why Everything About You Matters!

Legacy Now will give you a tridimensional purpose in life, helping you to focus daily on the *personal, generational,* and *eternal* perspectives of living.

Legacy Now shows you how to deal with the destiny in your DNA—the *character, charisma,* and potential *chaos* that are flowing in your bloodline.

Legacy Now explores how you can actually change your DNA/bloodline and how the principles of legacy can transform and conform your *iniquity* (the bad) into *equity* (the good) to perform positively for generations to come.

Legacy Now takes you on a step-by-step journey of building a legacy. This book is packed with practical ideas and action steps and contains compelling stories to illustrate the principles of a legacy:

- *Faith:* what you believe is what you will leave.

- *Family:* in every deed there is a seed.

- *Former life:* dealing with and healing iniquity.

- *Finances:* your treasure is not just for pleasure.

- *Future life:* living for generations to come.

*I dedicate this book to my grandchildren,
who are still behind the curtain waiting for the
perfect time to make an entrance into this world.*

Acknowledgments

It's intriguing observing a small remnant of moviegoers watch the credits roll at the end of a movie, waiting to see their names or the names of friends or family members (it's a Southern California thing). Seeing the shy grin spread across their faces into a full-grown smile is a tender moment of joy to behold. For those who have helped "produce" this book, may you have that same experience as the credits roll.

To Barbara Geraghty for your sacrificial effort. I know and God knows it was a labor of love. Your persistence and patience gently pushed me. Thank you.

Brent Roam, my godson, you make me proud, and your father is certainly grinning from heaven. You are brilliant, and allowing your thoughts and words to mate with mine has left your DNA in this book.

Eternal gratefulness to Mike Evans, Wes Beavis, the late Evelyn Roberts, Tommy Tenney, and Joel Osteen, who insisted that I write this book. Thanks to Frank Jones for the final "touch" of blessings. My church staff (especially Hodges Pickett and Jacob Rivers) and congregation at Life Church—you are the "cause and effect" of this book. To my literary agents Tom Winters and especially Jeff Dunn and to the Strang Communications team—you have made my first published book a true joy.

Having taken fourteen months to write this book, there are many others who walked in and out of this project, and while I'm certain I will have missed a few names unintentionally, your heavenly Father certainly and intentionally will bless you. (His rewards are more meaningful, anyway.)

The legacy of my family—my mom and dad, Frank and Ruth Munsey—you make me so proud to carry your DNA. To Odie and Maria and in memory of Vancie Coffey (my wife's mother), I love the DNA heritage I have received through covenant with your daughter. To my immediate family, Doug and Kara, without your support and sacrificial work, this book would be on yellow pads stuffed in some drawer in my office desk. Kara, you bring out the best in me because you are the best of me. This book doesn't happen without you. Period. Phillip II, you were the constant encourager. It was a reversal of roles—you fathered me through this book. Andrew, you were the iron that sharpened iron. How did you get so smart? Thanks for your "ministry" that got me through the late nights.

Jeannie, my love, my life, and the wife of my youth. I remain intrigued and in love with you—thirty years and counting. You transcend encouragement and support. You are both my coach and my biggest fan.

To Jesus Christ, who has given me the privilege of calling God "Father" and the empowering of the Holy Spirit. I have been adopted into the greatest legacy of all.

Contents

Part Three: Your Present

Part Four: Your Future

Legacy Confession of Life

God has made from **one blood** *all men to dwell on all the face of the earth, and through that blood, has determined* **when** *we were to be born,* **where** *we were to be born, in hope that we would seek Him and know the purpose of* **why** *we were born.*
—ACTS 17:26–27, AUTHOR'S PARAPHRASE

CHAPTER 1

The Generational– Driven Life

It's not just about you; it's not just about now!

ImaGENE: i-ma-gene; a fusion of our imagination and genetic possibilities.*

I IMAGINED...

I heard a tap on my office door. Thinking it was my secretary, I mumbled, "Come in!" The door opened, and I was nearly blinded by shafts of radiant light that burst into my office, bathing every shadow in a brilliant white glow. The sounds of a massive banquet outside the walls of my office tumbled into my ears: the tinkling of glasses, the ringing of silverware on china plates, laughter, and the gleeful squeals of children playing.

Shielding my eyes, I could make out the silhouette of a large, fit man who nearly filled the doorframe.

"Phil Munsey?" he inquired.

"Yes," I stammered, puzzled more than frightened.

"Come with me."

His voice was gentle, but the authority in his tone left no room for argument. I slowly rose to my feet. "Where are we going?" I meekly demanded.

---

* *ImaGENE* is a word I have coined to fuse the meaning of our imagination-belief in the invisible and the biology of genetics.

"Don't worry," he smiled. "You'll feel right at home." Then he turned and walked out the door. I stood for a moment longer; the sound of the massive party filled my office.

Unable to contain my curiosity, I walked into the light. As I crossed the threshold of my office door, my eyes adjusted to the radiance, and what I saw stretched before me would forever change my life.

I was standing in a huge banquet hall. The hall was packed literally with thousands of men, women, and children. They were gathered around long, opulent tables, feasting, laughing, celebrating, and greeting each other with hugs, handshakes, and hearty pats on the back.

Some were dressed like me; others wore ancient garb, tunics, kilts, togas, and robes; and some wore fashions I had never seen before. They were almost futuristic.

My host chuckled at the mesmerized stare on my face.

"Notice anything in particular?" he asked.

Then I saw it—a table right in the middle of the party. Seated at the table was my wife. To her left sat my two sons, and to her right were my daughter, her husband, and their families. Next to them were my parents and my siblings, and beside them were their parents and several others I did not recognize. There were children I had never seen before at the table, but I noticed they looked like me (poor little guys). They had my ears, my teeth, and my mischievous smile.

Chills ran down my spine.

This felt like déjà vu and destiny all at once.

"What's going on?" I inquired of my host. He smiled and turned toward the throng.

"Ladies and gentlemen!" his voice bellowed and echoed through the packed banquet hall. A hush settled over the multitude.

"Allow me to introduce someone you already know." Thousands of friendly eyes bore into me, welcoming and smiling.

"Who are these people?" I whispered to my host.

"This is your legacy, Phil. These are the men and women who came before you—your great-great-great-grandparents—and the men, women, and children who came after you—your great-great-great-grandchildren throughout all of time."

My mind felt as if it were being stretched like a rubber band.

"But there are so many," I said.

"Yes," he laughed, "and they've all been waiting for you to acknowledge them. Glad you could make it."

I stared back at the silent throng. So these were my people, as far back as Adam and as far forward as time itself. The magnitude of it overwhelmed me. I stood silently staring back at them.

I could hear my heart thumping in my chest and the thin, steady rhythm of air flowing in and out of my lungs.

"And who are you?" I asked, turning back toward my host.

But he was gone.

As quickly as it came, the vision vanished, and I was left sitting in my office, staring at the flecks of dust that float through the lamplight on my desk.

I want to take you on an adventure into the past, present, and future of your life, through the *eternal eyes* of legacy. This paradigm will open a whole new dimension to your life's purpose. Once grasped, legacy will lead you into the starring role of a drama for the ages, a role you will play out in your everyday actions and attitudes.

Legacy in the past has been associated with retirement, old age, legal wills, and the like. But that is not the case today. It is fast becoming a defining view of how we should live our lives now! Since the mapping of the genome, resulting in the completion of the "Genome Book of Life," we understand now more than ever the influence genetics has on our lives. As a result, it has become not only vital but thankfully vogue to live your life as if everything about you matters—because it does![2]

> I saw behind me those who had gone, and before me those who are to come. I looked back and saw my father, and his father, and all our fathers, and in front my son, and his son, and the sons upon sons beyond. And their eyes were my eyes.[1]
>
> —Richard Llewellyn

This discovery has science and Scripture surprisingly in harmony over the profoundness of the blood. This fresh revelation on the power and purpose of both Christ's blood and yours will strengthen and stretch your faith.

These new destiny-affecting secrets have never been revealed to any other generation. Never has a generation needed its faith confirmed more than now. Never has a generation needed its purpose more clearly defined.

Scientific discoveries have provided new and incredible information confirming the ancient scriptural teaching about the purpose of the blood. The Scriptures now look more like a science textbook, especially as it pertains to blood—the DNA of mankind.

Your life is connected to a distinctive bloodline. This is God's way of guaranteeing that a legacy—a life lived for generations to come—is possible. Legacy links us to the eternal purpose of God. The principles of legacy connect the dots and make sense out of what could otherwise seem senseless. Failures, frustrations, and the fatigue of life can be fused to something meaningful when viewed through a multigenerational mind-set. Your vision clears when aligned through the lens of legacy. Not only will your life's experiences find greater value, but the experiences of those who follow you will, too.

This phenomenon comes through the blood.

The blood has been "rediscovered" as a magnificent miracle!

Our blood cells "talk" through our DNA; they trace and transfer our personal history through generations.[3] Your attitudes and actions are mysteriously linked to your blood and will forever carry influence long after you are gone. My friend, everything about you matters!

The blood of Christ is also being "rediscovered" as a magnificent miracle.

The remarkably good news is that through this marvelous mystery of the blood of Christ, our iniquity—all our bad—can become HIStory. Even better news is that our equity—all our good—is being accumulated through us for the next generation. What is yet the greatest news is that our iniquity can actually become our equity.

Purpose asks us to understand why on earth we are here. Legacy asks us to grasp what on earth we will leave. Life is not just about how you live but what you leave. It's time to come to terms with our legacy opportunity—now!

We didn't plan our entrance into this world, and we can't avoid our exit.

When we face our lives' inevitable end, we are actually discovering the best place to begin. Facing our mortality is our first resurrection. The statistics on death are alarmingly sobering—one out of one human beings will die! Our prayer should be, "Let us *awake* before we *die* to our legacy."

How you live and what legacy you leave will determine the true worth of your life. I want our time together in this book to stir you to an eternal and generational perspective of life that will raise your genetic stock to its highest level.

For only as you see the eternal and generational view of your life will you experience the personal fulfillment you were meant to have.

WHAT IS A LEGACY?

Legacy is organizing the way you live your life so that you will be a blessing to other people for generations to come. It's nothing more (or less) than taking the responsibility to ensure that your relationships and resources will outlive and outlast your time on this earth.

Living without a legacy perspective is like watching a high-definition (HD) television program without a high-definition television set. Not only will it be blurry, but you will also miss the layered brilliance of the whole experience. Life will never be fully realized in the limited single dimension of just what is *personal*. Get past *you* and the *now*, for only when your life is viewed in the tridimensional of the *personal, generational*, and *eternal* together is life captured in high-definition vision.

> **Legacy is a strategic commitment to link your *resources* through covenantal *relationships* to your generational *responsibilities*, which will result in an eternal *reward*.**

Legacy is a desire with *instructions*, flowing with *inspiration* from God through your *imagination* and compelling you to leave an *impartation* beyond your lifetime.

5

I like the definition from the information technology industry. In IT, legacy software applications are those that have been inherited from earlier technology. The challenge is to keep the legacy application running, since it serves critical needs, while converting to newer and more efficient codes that utilize new technology.

Let's simplify this and apply it to your life. What did you inherit from your lineage that you want to keep running? What needs to be converted to newer, more efficient code?

God has made you the author of your own personal legacy and a contributing member to the legacies of others. Your legacy includes not only every person in your family's bloodline but also those with whom you have entered into covenant relationships. The people of your church, your community, the citizens of your country, and in some cases, even citizens in far-off lands may become intricately related to the legacy that you create, the legacy that extends from here to eternity. Whether you are a teenager, a single adult, a parent, a baby boomer, a senior citizen, a grandparent, a widow, or an orphan, you have a legacy—a legacy that you are creating even this very moment.

Everything about you matters! Every trial, test, and triumph is not just personal, but generational with eternal consequences.

Your life is more than a chain of events; it's a part of a chain that links you to the eternal purpose of God. This purpose comes to you and through you by and large from your genes. Don't worry if you feel that you have some bad blood running through your hereditary veins. There is a transformation transfusion available for you to fix that. Just know that it has taken generations to bring you to where you are today. Your worth and responsibility are significant. Life is not just for living; it's also for leaving a legacy. God intends for and depends on you to fulfill this mandate.

LIVING FOR GENERATIONS TO COME

I live in the canyons of Orange County, California. There is only one road leading from my home to my church, and it passes one of the largest churches in the nation. Saddleback Church, under Pastor Rick Warren, has grown to twenty-thousand-plus people in weekly attendance. He is the author of *The Purpose-Driven Life*, which has become the best-selling nonfiction hardback book in history.[4]

On many Sunday mornings, while trying to get to my church for the early morning service, I've waited behind hundreds of cars lined up to go to Saddleback Church. I've been tempted to put a sign on my car that reads, "Follow me to preferred parking," and then proceed to take them to the church my wife and I pastor (Life Church).

I can't even get a gallon of milk without passing Saddleback Church. Many times I have been overwhelmed with feelings of discouragement, jealousy, and even anger. Believe me, there were days when it was a battle to even look at Saddleback Church.

Finally, I couldn't take it anymore. I asked God, "Why is Pastor Rick getting all the blessings? Why do twenty thousand people go to Saddleback, and we have less than two thousand people on our best week? Can't You spread the love?"

I know this sounds so superficial, but, hey, I was down and pouting.

This was the moment God chose to reveal the concept of legacy to me. He spoke to my heart: "How will you feel if one of your children or grandchildren is raised up to build a church with the kind of influence that you see in Saddleback Church? What if your daughter or grandson writes a book that touches millions? How will you feel about that?"

At that time, I was not aware that Pastor Rick Warren is a fourth-generation preacher. Kay, his wife, is a preacher's kid with a similar legacy. God has used legacy in the Warren family to connect faithfulness from one generation to another. Rick and Kay are the latest link in a legacy that has been accumulating favor and blessings.

God was saying, "Everything matters, Phil!" All my efforts and sacrifices, though they may appear seemingly insufficient, were accumulating toward the ongoing purpose of God. My life has value that can't be measured by the limited standards of the here and now!

If I am willing to stay focused and faithful, there is no telling what could become of this legacy. My life and lineage are limited only by my imaGENEation.

This moment of humility showed me the honor I would feel to be a strong link in a multigenerational legacy. This was the moment I decided that quitting is never an option. I realized that everything I do today matters from a generational perspective.

You may be the first in your lineage, as far as you know, committed to living a life beyond just you and beyond just for today. You may be the one called to be a trailblazer that plows a path for the generations to come. There will be no signs along the way for you to follow. Only God goes before you. You may feel alone, but be assured many will follow.

Throughout this book we will visit the lineage of many. Their stories are meant to inspire, not intimidate. As I wrote this book, I was constantly reminded that while many of you will come to a greater appreciation of your lineage, others of you might experience feelings of awkwardness and even shame. Don't!

Every great and godly legacy starts with one person. Someone who says, "Enough is enough." No more pointless pain. No more tolerance for the deceitful, destructive, and dysfunctional lifestyle. Time to reverse the curse. Will that someone be you?

With a generational-driven life, I now see my purpose through eternal eyes. The external pressures and measures of others will no longer intimidate me. I will not allow myself to be haunted by internal comparisons with others. The eternal perspective—*not* the external or internal—will drive my passion and purpose.

YOUR BEST LEGACY NOW

Chances are, you have probably heard of Joel Osteen. Joel is the pastor of Lakewood Church, and he preaches in the former Compaq Center in Houston, Texas. (He's that smiling preacher you see on television.) His book *Your Best Life Now: 7 Steps to Living at Your Full Potential* has sold over five million copies.[5]

Joel and I have talked many times about legacy and the impact it has had on him and his family. Joel was one of my friends who insisted that this message and the passion that God has placed in my heart be put in a book. We both feel that too often people give up on their dream too soon, simply because they lose sight of a generational perspective. Your life matters. Everything you say and do is a deposit into your legacy.

Joel and Victoria, along with the whole Osteen family, have become a clear example of what a legacy looks like. Joel's father, John Osteen, founded the church in a feed store on Mother's Day 1959. Everyone said the church would fail because of the bad location and squalid environment. As a result of his faith in his mission, John and his wife, Dodie, developed Lakewood Church into a body of approximately six thousand members with an active television ministry, crusades, conferences, missionary support, and food distribution.

John always said, "God will raise up somebody to preach when I'm gone." Joel listened and thought, "Yeah. God's gonna raise somebody up." He was young and completely content producing his father's television program. He had absolutely no desire to preach.

In 1999, John died unexpectantly of a heart attack. Shortly after going through the loss of his father, Joel knew God was leading him to take over the church. He had only preached once in his life—*the week before his father's death!*

For the first year, Joel would take the shoes of his father and slip them on before each time he would speak. It would be the perfect reminder not only that he needed the strength of his father but also of the responsibility of his parents' legacy that he was stepping into. Then, expressing the greatest compliment that could ever be bestowed on any parent, Joel placed his father's shoes aside and stepped into his own shoes. The transfer was complete.

Joel reflects to our generation the power of a legacy. He continuously honors the legacy seeds that were sown into his life by his parents' fifty-year commitment to ministry. He literally stepped into his father's shoes, and like all godly legacies, he stepped up to a higher level.

I asked Joel many times what it felt like to walk through that sacred yet potentially dangerous transition. His answer is always the same: "Phil, I just knew in my knower that everything was going to be all right. I just knew!"

The greatest attribute that I see in Joel is his innocent and pure confidence that he is doing what God has called him to do. I never met his father. Joel and I became friends after John's death. I'm envious when I hear those who knew John talk about this great man. I see the spark in their eyes as they speak of his kindness and grace, his positive faith and his love for all people.

But when I watch Joel's passion to help bring healing to people who have been hurt, when I hear him say, "I just want to give people the good news; I want to give people hope," I see his daddy. When I watch Joel sign books for hours, always ready to bring a smile to people's hearts, I see John. When he takes time to show his love to the people who stop him on the streets, when he refuses to publicly judge people with blanket statements that show no regard of each individual person's situation, when I see the tears that flow from Joel's sensitive spirit, I see his father's heart. Yeah, I guess I know John—I know him in Joel.

When you've seen the son, you've seen the father.

Lakewood Church is now the largest church in the nation. More than being a large church—it's a legacy church. Lakewood Church is enjoying the fruit of the seeds of sacrifice, success, and succession sown for a legacy.

> Each generation goes further than the generation preceding it because it stands on the shoulders of that generation. You will have opportunities beyond anything we've ever known.
>
> —Ronald Reagan

The question every parent, teacher, coach, or entrepreneur needs to ask himself or herself is: Am I a John Osteen or a Joel Osteen? Is my role to sacrifice for the next generation? Am I a steward of the success given to me by the sacrifice paid by those before me? Am I playing my role in the perpetuation of a legacy?

Every sacrifice matters!

I once saw a bumper sticker on the back of an expensive recreational vehicle that read, "We're spending our children's inheritance!" Funny but tragic! What have you done this year, this week, today to provide material for the next generation to build the legacy God has mandated?

THE LEGACY GOD HAS MANDATED

As you hold this book in your hand, I want you to know that you also hold a legacy in your heart. This book will utilize principles and guidelines to prepare you to live and leave a legacy. "For our light affliction, which is but a moment, is working for us a far more exceeding and eternal weight of glory, while we do not look at the things which are seen, but at the things which are not seen. For the things which are seen are temporary, but the things which are not seen are eternal" (2 Cor. 4:17–18).

I have an important announcement for you. God is up to something in your life! How do I know this? You are reading this book.

You may be hearing a little voice in your head saying, "Oh, I doubt it. Certainly God can find someone more accomplished than me to do His work."

By the way, you may be thinking, "What little voice?"

That's the one!

PART ONE

Your Foundation

What you believe is what you will leave. Your faith becomes the foundation for those who follow you to build a legacy upon.

CHAPTER 2

Biology of Belief
What in the DNA are we talking about?

If anyone is in Christ, he is a new creation; old things have passed away; behold, all things have become new.
—2 CORINTHIANS 5:17

HISTORY IS PACKED WITH STORIES OF INDIVIDUALS WHOSE LIVES OF decadence, depravity, doubt, and depression were radically altered by a single moment, a moment when they chose to believe. Consider these questions: Could belief be wired into your biology? What if your spiritual beliefs actually cause a change in your blood? What if faith changes your DNA and therefore affects your lineage? What if your destiny is in your DNA?

If you could make yourself taller, leaner, healthier, more athletic, or better looking by thought alone, wouldn't you do it? That may not be possible, but it is possible to change your life and the lives of thousands of your descendants by altering the beliefs you hold about God, yourself, and others.

BELIEF THAT CHANGES BEHAVIOR

Rudy was born and raised in a very strict, religious home. Activities such as watching television, playing sports, and even attending Cub Scouts were forbidden. His father required that he memorize entire chapters of the Bible, and Rudy would be pulled by his ear to the altar and made to stay there until the end of the service for an infraction—not a positive

15

experience. His perception of God was, "This is what it is." He certainly had no intention of carrying on that kind of tradition.

When he was sixteen, he started sneaking out at night to party and drink. As a young man, he pursued his childhood desire of becoming a fireman. This had several positive motivations. It carried prestige, freedom from his parents' heavy-handed control, and Rudy was into the fire department's "Work hard—play hard" culture. Rudy loved the work, and he loved to party.

When he was twenty-three, he met a beautiful young lady named Julie at a Christian function. She came from a religious background but had embraced it all the way. Rudy was drawn to her positive and pure heart and intended to have a godly wife while he himself would live an ungodly life.

And when she accepted his proposal, he figured he had it made.

Shortly after they married, Julie realized they were definitely not on the same page with God. There were some troubling issues stirring in their relationship. The marriage was becoming more about endurance than enjoyment.

By the time their daughters became teenagers, their marriage began to unravel. Rudy chose heavy drinking as a coping strategy, and all Julie could do was pray (not a bad option). On a typical Sunday, Rudy would watch sports and get drunk while Julie took the girls to church. Theirs was not a happy marriage. To protect their daughters from the growing tension, they would often do their fighting in the car. It wouldn't matter. All could see and know that this marriage was in trouble.

Finally, Julie called her mother and spiritual mentor and told them, "I'm at the end of my rope. Be prepared for the end. Our marriage is not going to make it."

One night, she went into the bathroom and buried her face in a pillow so her daughters would not hear her crying. She wept bitterly and painfully in her prayer to God. To her amazement, she found herself holding out for hope that somehow something would change. "I can't believe this is what You want for me. I am miserable, and he is a horrible example for the girls. But if this is what You want, I'll stay married to him," she told God.

A deal was struck. She told Rudy that all she asked was that he would at least go to church with her. Rudy went all right—with a closed mind, a critical heart, and crossed arms. A few months later, he asked Julie what she wanted for Valentine's Day, and of all things, she wanted him to take her to a Valentine's party at church. This was not what Rudy had in mind.

Rudy was thinking a fancy dinner or jewelry; this would not be a fun time. He decided, "The only way I can deal with this is to be buzzed."

So before they left for the banquet, he drank as much and as fast as he could to help him survive the night. Worse yet, he began unleashing venom about the church and the pastor (that would be me).

I remember seeing Rudy sitting at the table, all grim-faced and miserable. I walked over to his table and put my hands on his shoulders and said, "This is a good man sitting right here." I was surprised when he stood up and hugged me, because that didn't seem like his style!

What influence was he under?

Rudy told me later that when he heard my words, something quickened inside him, but all he could think was, "You don't know me. I'm a bad person."

The evening ended seemingly without much drama.

> **Sometimes all it takes for someone to believe is for someone to believe in them.**

But as soon as he got in the car with Julie to go home, Rudy started sobbing. She had never seen him cry before. He cried all the way home. He kept saying, "To think that the Creator of the universe would care about me."

When they got home, Rudy was praying, and he and Julie were hugging when she felt *a physical change come over his body*!

The next morning when he woke at 4:00 a.m. to go to the fire station, Rudy knelt down beside the bed and prayed for Julie. That one single moment set off a destiny of generational proportions.

This is just one story of the hundreds of millions of people who through simple faith see their lives changed in an instant.

That is the power of belief!

Christians are people who have experienced a life-changing transformation. It is more than an acceptance of a religious system. It is more than a decision to try to be or do better. Something miraculous happens when we pray that simple prayer. A blood transformation—*transmutation*—of DNA is triggered.* You read right. True belief conforms our behavior by transforming our biology.

Conversion is not a process of small mental ascents that come by our will power. We're talking about a "twinkling of an eye" change. We immediately begin acting different because we *are* different!

What's more, that choice gives you a voice into the lives of those in your lineage. The difference will be felt for generations to come. Your behavior transformation becomes transferable through your blood.

Why Blood?

The examples of the use of blood in the Old Testament begin the intrigue about the significant power of the blood. Why would the blood play such a role in the covenants God made with mankind?

These are some examples of the significant power of the blood in the Old Testament:

- The sacrificial blood offering that God accepted from Abel (Gen. 4:4)

- The sacrificial offering by Noah after the flood (Gen. 8:20)

- Abraham's animal sacrifice that confirmed the covenant (Gen. 15:9–18)

- The animal sacrifices of the tabernacle of Moses, David, and Solomon (Heb. 9:18–22)

From the very beginning, God has shown us that the wages of sin are death (Rom. 6:23). When Adam and Eve disobeyed God in the garden, the skins of animals were used to cover their shame and sin (Gen. 3:21).

There is always a cost to pay for sin; someone, somewhere, at some time will pay.

---

* *Transmutation*: the conversion of one element or nuclide into another either naturally or artificially.

Sin is a violation against God. Sin separates us from God.

The shedding of blood was required as payment for sin. The blood represented the cost of the sin committed. Sin demands a penalty of death. The blood from animal sacrifices was only the *credit* applied for mankind's sin. Man was given a credit card—religion—and began laying up a huge debt that cost Christ dearly. It took the precious and perfect blood of Christ, which was shed on the cross, to redeem us and pay our sin debt in full.

All of the emphasis on the blood pointed to what would be needed to heal and deal with the tainted blood that we all inherited through Adam. We would all need atonement for our sins. Christ's blood became the ultimate "at-one-ment" that would unite our hearts back to God.

Tom Riles, a friend of mine, has a disease that causes him to produce too many red blood cells. This life-threatening disease has exposed him to the need hospitals have for blood donors. As a result, Tom has started an organization called "Save 3 Lives Today," which encourages people to donate blood, which literally can save lives. *USA Today* has even featured his story.[1]

Lizzie, a fifth grader who loves to dance, has Diamond-Blackfan anemia, a rare bone-marrow disease that only seven hundred people worldwide have been diagnosed with. She would die without twice-monthly blood transfusions. Lizzie's mother made contact with Tom when she read his story. The little girl needs a transfusion to replace the blood in her that doesn't make any red blood cells. Tom needs to rid himself of blood that makes too many red blood cells. The exchange that they both submit to is saving their lives.

Our lives need saving, too.

We produce too many *sin* blood cells. Christ has blood that is "spotless." Daily we come to the place of grace to receive this transfusion: "…with the precious blood of Christ, as of a lamb without blemish and without spot" (1 Pet. 1:19).

THE TRANSFORMING TRANSFUSION

As early as the fifteenth century, doctors began to realize that life, death, sickness, and health reside in the blood. In 1667 Richard Lower and Jean-Baptiste Denis reported successful transfusions from lambs (how ironic!) to humans.[2] Since then, science has advanced to such a degree that blood transfusions are successfully performed routinely, and millions of lives are saved annually as a result.

To those unfamiliar with the language and images of Christianity, all the talk of blood must sound gruesome and alarming. But is it any wonder that God would choose the very wellspring of our lives to be the source of our salvation?

For thousands of years in cultures all around the globe, the act of bloodletting has been linked to the appeasement of cultural deities. In Mesoamerica, the Aztecs made human sacrifices to their god, Huitzilopochtli, to insure that the sun would rise the following day.[3]

The Romans, the Greeks, and the Yoruba in Africa have all been known to ritually sacrifice animals as part of their religious practice.

So, when looked at through the lens of history, it does not seem so odd that God would choose to redeem the world by sending His only begotten Son to be sacrificed. Christ became the eternal and ultimate sacrifice, whose blood covered the sins of men, women, and children for all times, tribes, and territories. Through the shedding of Christ's blood, God has redeemed the sins of the entire world. The divine nature of the Son of God redeemed the divisive nature of man.

Is there more to understand about the blood than we've known before?

What if the biblical concept of "the blood saves" is more than a type, a shadow, or an analogy? What if conversion is not just a spiritual event but also a *transformation that is both a biblical and biological truth*? What if we are saved by the blood of Christ not only in the spiritual sense but also by a *literal* change at the moment of salvation? What if the Bible was pointing to the future—now—when we could really understand just how magnificently the blood works?

We stand to miss powerful truths when we look at just the limited typology of animal sacrifices expressed in Old Testament times. Today we can draw from breakthrough scientific knowledge, which brings innumerable insights into why God placed our redemption in the blood. The better covenant we have in Christ is, no doubt, the revelation of the ways, works, and wonders of the blood.

This truth was restricted to "types and shadows" in the Old Testament. Even though the sacrifice of animals served as a very descriptive type of the purpose of the blood, it has always been just that—a type! The time has come for this generation to take the power of the blood out of the shadows and into the light. The saving power of the blood that I grew up singing about intrigues me beyond the "types and shadows"!

Life really *is* in the blood (Lev. 17:11). Blood is the main ingredient of every living, breathing human creation of God. Its vein-pulsing flow invigorates and sustains the very gift of physical existence. Its presence inside a body is the ultimate evidence of life. If enough blood spills out of the body, life ceases.

> **When your beliefs change your behavior, your faith achieves a biological wonder that will be transferred into the DNA of the next generation!**

Realizing the value of this life-giving flow, God chose the element of blood as the currency for His arrangement with the sins of man. With its complex makeup of over four hundred known ingredients, this miraculous mix cannot be duplicated by any man-made substitute. DNA sampling is slowly revealing the magnificent ways of man made known through the blood. Real core change would not come by man's will but by the working of the blood of Christ. That wonderful work is not just an analogy!

If who we are comes through our DNA, then the power to become new creations, as believers, must find a way to be infused into our DNA. I contend that it does!

All right, don't worry that we are going to get bogged down in scientific jargon. I'm not that smart. But the credibility and key characteristic of building a legacy is linked to our DNA and how it works in securing the plan of God for making our lives count for generations.

THE BIOLOGY OF BELIEF

The fact that not all human beings look identical is the result of subtle variations or *mutations* in our DNA, which account for the differences in our looks as well as more serious hereditary changes and diseases.

These DNA mutations are passed down from parent to offspring.[4] Our DNA contains information about processes that occurred in the past, processes what happens today, and carries that information into the future. The collective deeds and demeanors of our ancestors comprise a great deal of who we are and how we will react to the world, which, of course, our offspring inherit.

When DNA was first discovered, it was called *transforming cells*, in part because the cells are capable of transforming or duplicating themselves. Given the proper "host" cells, any number of transformations through these cells is possible. Can the Spirit of God serve as the Holy "Ghost" cell that brings supernatural change? Can it take what is initially a belief and turn it into a biological transformation?

I believe it might be discovered someday that the DNA structure of a believer is noticeably different after conversion. I think it is possible that conversion recalibrates the genetic code and allows you to rebuild parts of your nature. I see DNA as a possible acronym for **D**ivine **N**ature **A**cquired!

> You may be partakers of the *divine nature*.
> —2 PETER 1:4, EMPHASIS ADDED

> Since we are *the offspring of God*, we ought not to think that the *Divine Nature* is like gold or silver or stone, something shaped by art and man's devising.
> —ACTS 17:29, EMPHASIS ADDED

With only about one-third of the human genome identified, scientists lack the understanding of the identity of the other two-thirds. Just a few years ago, the scientific community called these genes "junk" DNA. Certainly, God doesn't make any junk!

They remain a mystery—to science!

I know it's a little edgy, but what if there is a faith gene? This could be an *assurance policy* that offers an inheritance to our descendants through the DNA-encoded bloodline of our lineage.

In the New Testament, the Bible offers the redemptive plan of God through access to the sinless blood of Christ through faith (Heb. 10:19–22).

Let's take the story of the birth of Jesus and look at it from a modern-day view.

> The Holy Spirit will come upon you, and the power of the Highest will overshadow you.
>
> —Luke 1:35

Mary was overshadowed (which means "to envelop in a haze of brilliancy; to invest with preternatural influence") by the Holy Spirit, and she allowed the Spirit of God to pierce the wall of her womb with the cell that carried the nature of the Christ child.

In a similar—but not exact—overshadowing, could the Holy Spirit birth in us a "seed" at the moment of salvation?

> **The truth of faith cannot be confirmed by the latest physical or biological or psychological discoveries—as it cannot be denied by them.**[5]
>
> **—Paul Tillich**

> You have been regenerated (born again), not from a mortal origin (seed).
>
> —1 Peter 1:23, amp

This would be a phenomenal *sign*, and it would certainly make us *wonder* about the power of belief.

> No one born (begotten) of God [deliberately, knowingly, and habitually] practices sin, for God's nature abides in him [His principle of life...] he is born (begotten) of God.
>
> —1 John 3:9, amp

This could not have been explained back at the time of Christ's ministry on Earth. It would not have been understood until now.

Francis Crick's and James Watson's discovery of the DNA structure fifty years ago marked one of the great turning points in the history of science.[6] Biology, immunology, medicine, and genetics have all been radically transformed as a result. I believe this is a sign for our generation!

From a gene pool of over thirty thousand genes, which have a variance into the millions, there could very well be a faith gene. This would explain the spirituality that seems to be part of our basic human inheritance. Science appears to be close to identifying that "faith" gene, which I believe is activated at the moment of genuine conversion. This transforming gene could be what creates a radical change in the life of a believer. What happens when a person comes to believe that Christ was God's Son and that God raised Him from the dead? When we offend our mind with that belief, might we at the same time trigger and fire into action a faith gene that would transcend belief to biology?

> **Could it be that at the moment we confess with our mouths and believe in our hearts, we "cross" the line of our limited intellect and tap into a dimension of faith that pierces the genetic wall and a true genetic mutation occurs?**

Is being born again an analogy, or is it something more?

And what if our destiny is linked to our DNA?

THE DNA LADDER TO PURPOSE

The field of genetics is making a very interesting biological connection between our destiny and our DNA. New developments are opening a window to a clearer view of what God always had in His plans for our lives.

DNA is the biological key that unlocks the mystery of why we are who we are. Everything, from the color and texture of our hair down to the size of our feet, is determined before we enter this world. The shape of our hands is out of our hands. DNA's genetic programming constructs the foundation of our character. All of our potential and many of our problems are contained in our individual DNA.

The "Genome Book of Life" that we each have contains one billion words. If it was put in print, it would equal the size of eight hundred Bibles. If this "book" were read at the rate of one word per second, eight hours a day, it would take one hundred years to read. This document fits inside the microscopic nucleus of a tiny cell that fits easily upon the head of a pin. The single DNA strand of the billions of people who have lived since Adam could be contained in three tablets the size of aspirin.[7]

God has managed to create an entire human race, billions of unique people, from matter that would barely fill one test tube.

The discovery of the DNA code provides a new perspective of our lives. DNA (deoxyribonucleic acid) is the blueprint of our being. Each cell is believed to carry all the information necessary to construct the entire body and encode all genetic information to build a life. The DNA double-helix strand stretches six feet, yet it is so small it can be lost on the top of a pinhead.

Like Jacob's spiraling ladder from the earth to heaven, the DNA staircase connects us to our God-given and God-driven life. Our DNA was designed to serve the intention of God by allowing the equity of mankind to be transferred to future generations for His eternal purpose.

Our destiny *is* in our DNA. Our blood carries this fascinating potential. Today, with this new understanding, we can have a fresh revelation of why the terms and insistent biblical use of blood carry meaning to everything about our lives.

Let's begin looking at this revolutionary concept by examining the transforming "cell" that came through Jesus Christ. Long before science knew, Christ would show us just how potent our bloodline is.

THE ORIGINAL LEVI GENES

Jesus became the ultimate mediator, a priest for all who would believe in Him. For those not familiar with the biblical account of how the priesthood was first established, a brief history may be necessary.

Levites were the original priests in the Old Testament. Moses was told by God to appoint the sons of Levi, one of the twelve tribes of Israel, to serve as priests in the temple.

Many centuries later, Christ would become our one and only eternal perfect priest. Christ would represent the original "Levi genes" that became our rightful inheritance to our own legacy.[8] The Gospels of

Matthew and Luke give us a look at the stock and genes of Jesus Christ. What a stock of genes they were!

There were great leaders, successful entrepreneurs, scholars, farmers, and preachers, many of whom were quite impressive and had outstanding character. Others were quite the characters. Liars, thieves, adulterers, prostitutes, and con artists. There were the single moms, the divorced, the widowed, the orphaned, the adopted, and the blended and broken families.

Dirty genes, wrinkled and worn-out genes, blue (depressed) genes, stained and ripped genes. From the functional to the dysfunctional, the wise to the witless. From the prosperous to the poverty stricken, there was every gene imaginable! In spite of their spite, everyone and their genes mattered. Everyone contributed to the greatest legacy ever—the legacy of Jesus Christ.

If for no other reason, when we observe the genealogy of Christ, we can at least feel comfortable in our own genes. But could there be a greater value in what Christ did with the genes that He came into this world with?

Jesus Christ was both the Son of God and the Son of man. As the old-time preachers would say, "Very God of God and very man of man!"

Christ was God manifested in the flesh. That means among many other great truths that Christ was fully human yet fully divine. Yet He chose to live His life as a man. Limited by the same restrictions that we may have considered too difficult to deal with, Christ showed us how we can take what we see as bad and turn it around into something good. Christ is our High Priest who knows completely how it feels to carry the baggage of dirty genes that would seem to dictate desired possibilities.

In her song "If God Was One of Us," Joan Osbourne ponders what God would have been like.

Well, God *did* become one of us! But why?

As a man, why did He need to come through a specific genealogy?

Did Christ's genes play a role in the fulfillment of His destiny— was He carrying genetic information that would prove vital in helping fulfill His divine mandate? Or were Jesus's ancestors simply a random assortment of arbitrary individuals?

We'll look at a few of these fascinating characters throughout the book. Let's begin with one of five women who give us some clues to just why everyone mattered and why everything about them mattered.

We begin with Tamar.

Tamar's husband died before they conceived a child. In the custom of the day, when a woman's husband died, she became the wife of her husband's brother. The brother was responsible for conceiving a child with her so that she could have someone to care for her in her old age and also so she could carry on her legacy. Oman, the elder brother, refused. Tamar's father-in-law, Judah, promised that he would give another of his sons to fulfill that promise, but it never happened. Instead, Judah disgraced Tamar by sending her back to her father.

Tamar, however, refused to be cast aside. She disguised herself as a temple prostitute and made herself available to her father-in-law, Judah. Because Judah did not have money with him at the time of the visit, Tamar claimed his cloak, his signet, and his staff in lieu of payment, never letting him discover her true identity.

As a result of their liaison, Tamar became pregnant. Judah, eager to rid himself of the responsibility he owed his former daughter-in-law, called for her execution, accusing her of fornication. But Tamar, a dozen steps ahead of her hypocritical father-in-law, came to him privately and handed him the signet, the cloak, and the staff. "The children [she would have twins] that you want to kill are your own," she said. Humbled and repentant, Judah took Tamar as his wife and cared for her the rest of his days. (See Genesis 38.)

Tamar's characteristics of tenacity, courage, and perseverance were certainly passed down to her great-great-great-grandchild Jesus! Is it not conceivable that Jesus would need these inherited traits to become the lowly servant who was rejected and despised so that He could ensure a godly legacy for you and me?

In the garden, Christ prayed with great sweatlike blood running down His face. He triumphed over fear to do the will of the Father. He found the strength and stamina to endure the suffering of the cross.

The blood that Christ perspired during His deep intercession carried the DNA from a rejected and despised woman who took on the role of a prostitute so that her legacy would continue. Tamar's determined DNA would not be denied its rightful inheritance. Perhaps her determination was passed on to Christ so that He would have the character to match His mandate. Just as Tamar humbled herself in the veil of a prostitute to ensure that her legacy would survive, so Christ veiled Himself in the garment of a lowly carpenter so that in the suffering of the cross, He could secure a legacy for you and me.

And what characteristics did her nearly executed son Perez develop that would be of use to Christ? Perez endured the sneers and whispers about his mysterious and unlawful birth. He, no doubt, was aware of the rumors swirling around about his dubious parentage. Yet he maintained his composure, brushing aside the scandalmongers. And his noble disposition was passed down through generations to his great-great-great-grandson Jesus, whose parentage was also the source of scandal, rumor, and innuendo.

The lives of Tamar and Perez are only two of many examples of how Christ's ancestors displayed specific traits that were useful to Jesus in His most difficult hours on Earth. I find it very unlikely that God populated His Son's human ancestry with random and arbitrary individuals. Rather, it seems far more likely that Christ's genealogy equipped Him with the requisite human characteristics to face His battles and fulfill His destiny.

Each person that came before Him contributed to the mix of highly specialized traits that Christ would need to fulfill His mission. Even what looks like utter failure can be used in a lineage that understands the power of faith in the blood of Christ. As each of His ancestors responded to their own personal struggles, they became links in a divine chain of events that would mean something, somewhere, at some special moment in the eternal legacy of Christ! Believe me when I tell you that *everything about you matters*!

This understanding places front and center what this book's message is all about. Everyone matters. Everything matters. At some point, every attitude and action of your life matters. If no one sees or acknowledges the seeds you've sown, they will still be shown in someone at someplace at sometime.

The most encouraging aspect of this revelation is that imperfect people played vital roles in the making of the perfect Man. God used their DNA and eliminated the wickedness, yet elevated the goodness, so that Christ could be the perfect Man. We are "joint heirs" in the ongoing legacy of Christ. Our lives serve the purpose of God on this earth. Our DNA, in spite of its imperfections, serves to protect and project the determined plans of God. Don't throw out your "genes" no matter how torn and worn they look.

THE DESTINY IN YOUR DNA

I will show you how God's intentions are perpetuated and accumulated throughout the generations. We will discover how everything we do is "affected" both retroactively and proactively in our lineage. *This does not give us excuses for our behavior, but it does offer some explanations.* These are laws of nature—not to limit you and me, but to line us up for the untapped potential waiting to be released in our lives.

Your destiny is encoded in your DNA. The access and ability to fulfill your destiny is also in your DNA. Take stock in your heritage. Therein you will find the inventory you need to succeed. Don't fight it. Let it work for you.

> **The blood is the carrier of our deeds, and nothing we do will go unnoticed, not only in the eternal but also in the generational!**

Nature and nurture are the twin engines that will take you to your divine destination. Both are there to be your master or your servant. The choice is up to you.

My youngest son, Andrew, a student at Southern California School of the Arts, initially rejected this idea that a person's destiny is connected to their DNA. (Ironically, where he got his aggressiveness to question things adds credibility to this premise. I was notorious for debating everything—I mean everything!) It felt restrictive to him and unfair that anyone would suggest that his life was not a blank page on which to write whatever dreams and desires he had.

I am certain that others might feel the same. But the point is not that you are limited by your DNA but rather that you are loosed to become all you were designed to be, released to be what you were called to be—not restricted.

Look at the value of everything you received in your nature as if it were a piece of steel. The piece of steel worth five dollars can be made into horseshoes and become worth ten dollars. If you manufacture sewing needles from that same piece of steel, the price rises to three hundred fifty dollars. What if you go to the limit and create springs to power Rolex watches? The value of your piece of steel just surged to two hundred fifty thousand dollars. The raw material remained the same—steel.

The value is contained in how you utilize the potential of the raw material—your DNA—that you have been given. The nature you have received does not restrict you. Nor is it a matter of nature versus nurture.

It is nature *via* nurture, and it is up to you to nurture the nature you've been given.

Nature Via Nurture

There is a continuous controversy over the relative impact of nature (genetics) versus nurture (environment) in our lives. How much of our lives is influenced by our nature—our DNA—and how much is determined by nurture—our environment?

When we say "environment," we're referring to a wide spectrum of factors. The environment includes everything—the color of the wallpaper in your bedroom as an infant, the gifts you received on your birthday, and your parents' income. It's the classes you took in school and the movie you watched last night. The environment is anything and everything—biological, physical, and intellectual—that you didn't inherit as DNA.

This controversy is best explored by comparing identical twins that were separated at birth and raised apart from each other. Because these identical twins share the same genes but are nurtured differently, the extent to which they are similar to each other is a direct result of matching DNA. Scientists can use this information to isolate the roles of genes and environment in human behavior.[9]

Twenty years ago, the University of Minnesota did what became a revolutionary study on families who had birthed twins.[10] The study investigated the lives of twins who were separated at birth. The research provides remarkable data that would expand the knowledge of genetic influence. The similarities between the twins were startling. They included specific habits, style of dress, favorite hobbies, using the same obscure brand of toothpaste, naming their children the same names, marrying spouses with the same first name, and even having the same religious preference.

My purpose is not to focus on resolving the issue of nature versus nurture. But I do believe Scripture places strong emphasis on nature's role (DNA) in our destiny.

Long after the effects of nurture, and sometimes in spite of them, the potent power of the blood "cries out" with influence that transcends our nurturing. *The longevity of our DNA's influence will last beyond that of nurture, especially when it comes to our lineage.*

HAND-ME-DOWN GENES

Golf is one of my passions, although my handicap of eighteen is truly a handicap. Recently, I went golfing with my boys, Phillip II, Andrew, and my son-in-law, Doug. Golfing together is a rare treat. Since they have grown up, getting all of us together at one time is quite an accomplishment.

Everyone was interested and engaged; we laughed, joked, and competed against one another in a way only family can.

It wasn't until reflecting a few days later that it hit me. I remembered the unique approach that Phil II had to hitting his driver. Since he isn't a golfer, his style is unlike anything you would ever see on TV. Of all the players I've ever played with, only one other person has ever hit the ball like him—his grandfather!

My father has an approach with his driver that is more like a batter taking practice swings in anticipation of hitting a baseball being pitched to him. It's the weirdest thing! My son had never been golfing with my father in his life. And yet he has the exact same swing.

This is not just a coincidence or a random reaction. This is more than a particular golf style. It's part of the signs we need to pay attention to that show the hereditary influence we have on the lifestyles of our children—and their children. We have been designed to receive and pass on the character and characteristics of our family. This is more than amusing—it's amazing.

When we realize this power, we will live with a deeper sense of meaning. We become aware that, more than just a biological link to us, our children are linked to our behavior also. If we are unaware or don't really care about this distinction, we will create unnecessary problems for the next generation and limit many positive possibilities.

We have been placed here with "designer genes." God designed us in such a way that a line of credit—equity and/or iniquity—is at work through the currency of our blood. Equity is the accumulation of good we do in our lifetime. Iniquity is the bad—the unresolved strife or sins that are left for the next generation to deal with (Deut. 5:9).

Living just for ourselves and in the present is the lowest denominator of one's drive for success. When our lives are viewed from that one-dimensional perspective, we can become deceived, discouraged, and distracted, and can even diminish the purpose God has for us.

When we live our lives through a generational mind-set, we gain an eternal perspective that allows us to see everything differently. Your personal life makes more sense when placed in the tension of a generational and eternal view.

THE ULTIMATE CELL PHONE

The choices you make today will become the voice of the future in your bloodline.

Imagine yourself, everywhere you go, being locked hand-in-arm with your father or mother on one side and your son or daughter on the other. This imaginary picture represents the reality of DNA. How would you live your life differently if your father and son, or mother and daughter, were with you everywhere you went?

They are!

Everywhere you go—in all your actions and even your attitudes— you take the legacy of your parents and the potential legacy of your children with you. Through our blood, we are always connected to our lineage. We are the link between the lineage we inherit and the legacy we leave.

The more you know about your past and are aware of its equity and iniquity, the more you are able to link up with your life's power and purpose. As I've stated, life goes beyond just asking, "How on earth will I live?" The question is, "What on earth will I leave!"

What if you could go into the future fifty to sixty years from now? What if you could have a conversation with your great-great-grandchild? What if you could affect who he or she would become, from habits to decisions and even to morals? Envision contributing to the dreams your great-grandchildren would have for their lives and for their children.

This incredible possibility is not a plot twist in a science-fiction novel. It is the brilliant plan of God, who wants you to know that everything you do means something. Everything you do today will become part of your seed for generations to come. You are living and leaving a legacy right now. ImaGENE that!

Everything that pertains to our lives connects in some shape or form to the blood. The blood cells have more capacity and creativity than the latest cell phone you could buy. When you or someone else says, "Can you hear me now?" while talking on a cell phone, I want it to remind you to think about how much influence you have over your seed.

Picture yourself talking to your children, your grandchildren, and their children, saying through your blood, "Can you hear me now?"

Your DNA cries out into future generations. What will your blood be saying? What will you be adding to the lineage that is to come?

A few years ago there was a popular television show called *The Weakest Link*. Contestants were dismissed from the show with the humiliating phrase, "You are the weakest link. Good-bye!"

Every one of your actions matters.

I would like to propose a more uplifting contest in a much more important game. Why not become the *strongest* link in a lineage that will change the world?

A desire for living and leaving a legacy is a clear sign that you are willing to follow the uncharted waters of faith. Come on in; the water of your gene pool is wonderful!

CHAPTER 3

What You Believe You Leave

Legacy—don't leave Earth without it!

Generation after generation stands in awe of your work; each one tells stories of your mighty acts.
—Psalm 145:4, The Message

THERE COMES A TIME IN MOST PEOPLE'S LIVES WHEN THEY REALIZE that it's not just about them anymore. For some, this comes at an early age; a few unfortunate souls never get it. For many, it occurs when they have children. For others, midlife—the moment when they realize that there is more life behind them than ahead of them—is when they begin to take stock and ask some serious questions.

There are seventy-eight million baby boomers in America. One of them turns sixty every six seconds, and the youngest are quickly approaching fifty.[1] This has created a huge generational interest in midlife evaluation. We are all feeling that it is time to make a change.

The evaluation is bringing a transition from "me" to "we," from "take" to "give," and from a "more-is-less" to a "less-is-more" world-view. There is a culture shift happening to the baby boomers.

Gradually, then suddenly, a change has come.

German psychologist Erik Erikson called this shift the developmental stage of "Generativity vs. Stagnation."[2] This is when man becomes aware of the need to live beyond himself and begins the difficult task of leading a meaningful and useful life. Erikson claimed that when a person feels he has done nothing to help insure a better future for the generations to come, he begins to feel stagnant and ultimately sinks into despair.

Those of us who are boomers are beginning to sense that it's more important to *leave* a name than to just *make* a name. We are seeing a growing desire from this generation to leave the kind of values that can't be calculated by an accountant. A word that seemed more appropriate for *old people* has grown into our vocabulary.

That word?

Legacy!

Legacy is evolving into a popular buzzword. The pressure to prove everything to everybody is beginning to ease. We are beginning to take some of that load away from our daily grind. The weight is lifting; a lighter load seems more and more appealing every day.

It's a welcome wake-up call. Too many *boomers* have been seduced into a superficial lifestyle. That noise you hear is the "bang" from a generation's vain values gone bust.

Things are looking different from where we stand now!

And what about you? Do you sense a call to something more?

Are you bogged down with the weight of the mundane and mediocre?

Let's lose the weight!

> Lay aside every weight, and the sin which so easily ensnares us.
> —HEBREWS 12:1

Are you under pressure to fulfill meaningless obligations? Beware of the heavy duties that cheat you of the joys of life. Be light on your feet. When did you last dance to the dazzling songs that are playing from heaven's symphony? Will you dance with the duet of destinies—the "past and future" of your legacy? Legacy is playing your song.

Are you even listening to the music? There is a new song in the air. The ear to hear its melody is in the center of your h-*ear*-t! Your heart knows the rhyme and reason of legacy. Trust your heart.

You may be reading this book because your life doesn't feel as fulfilling or meaningful as it used to feel. You are looking for something more—or actually, less. Are you seeking a life with less stress, less distress, less of the "got-to-have-more" lifestyle, which is just not adding up?

The launching of a legacy does not always come in our timing or in our ways. The "times and the seasons" for our visitations sometimes come when we are not prepared for, or even seeking, a major life change (1 Thess. 5:1). When the time does come, the window of an open heaven offers a glimpse into a whole new world. Go for it! A legacy will awaken you to the original passion behind those distant dreams. You will again believe that the things that seem impossible can become possible!

Legacy appeals to the higher call and meaning we need in order to live a fulfilled life. When you hear that call, you will do well to heed it.

You may be at a place where you are asking some delightfully difficult questions. What have I accomplished with my life? I mean, really accomplished? What will stand after my life is over? If I had a chance to choose today, what would I want people to remember me for? What would I want them to say about the life I've lived after I'm gone?

Lou Holtz made this statement: "When I die and people realize that I will not be resurrected in three days, they will forget me."[3] (If you are a football fan, I'm certain you won't forget him.)

I don't think any of us should live by that premise. Your life came from God, and God put a calling on your life that includes the promise of a legacy. Legacy is not a luxury. It's not really even a choice—it's a consequence. God wants us to have an intellectual inquisitiveness that puts us on a search for the deeper and more meaningful purpose in life.

> That they should seek the Lord, in the hope that they might grope
> for Him and find Him, though He is not far from each one of us;
> for in Him we live and move and have our being.
> —Acts 17:27–28

Hope to grope? Sounds like something we would want to avoid!

Yet it is in your groping that you find Him—and in Him you find your true self. It is these moments of vulnerability that reveal God's presence and purpose to you. Groping for Him opens hope in your heart. It is that "hope" God is counting on you to "grope" after, for it will bring you to the place where "in Him we live and move and have our being."

That passion will be your link to living and leaving a legacy.

> But if we hope for what we do not see, we eagerly wait for it with perseverance...with groanings which cannot be uttered.
>
> —ROMANS 8:25–26

This "hope" is a groaning, a deep longing that can't be spoken or understood by logic alone. It is pulling you toward something very rewarding.

Listen.

Follow.

It will lead you home. You will never be more at home in your own skin than when you have groped—passionately pursued—your way to the eternal hope that is pounding in your heart. Your heart is where your home is!

At your heart's home will be the memories and pictures to remind you and even guide you through your journey. Go there. When you know where you've come from, you will know best where you need to go. Your life will be full of purpose, a life beyond yourself.

Legacy is, in some ways, the overflowing of your life spilling over to the next generation. In the words of the apostle Paul (who was single, according to Bible scholars, reminding us that *everyone* has a legacy): "I am already being poured out as a drink offering...my departure is at hand" (2 Tim. 4:6).

Ask yourself these questions:

- What is the best part of me that I want to be celebrated?

- What part of my life do I want to "spill over" to the next generation?

- What do I want my legacy to be?

See, wasn't that easy? Now you are asking the kind of questions that God just loves to answer. Stay in that place of prayer and imagination, and listen for the still, small voice to reveal God's intentions for your lineage and your legacy.

Your desire for a legacy just might be what God uses to bring you into His world of faith!

What desires do you have that might become the dream that grows into your legacy? All good desires come from our Father God above. The evil one likes to place his own counterfeit versions of his cynical and sinful desires in our minds (Eph. 2:2), but a pure heart clearly discerns the differ-

Every dream matters!

ence. The desires that God gives us are the seeds of dreams, needing only the light of God's Spirit and the water of His Word to nurture growth. The dreams come with instructions, which release an irrigation system when we commit our life to the purposes of God.

Your dream will come to full maturity within your legacy. A dream is a desired vision that becomes a solved problem to advance the plan of God. When a dream is fully realized, it becomes too virtuous to be done alone and too noble to be accomplished in one's lifetime.

> Trust in the LORD, and do good…
> Delight yourself also in the LORD,
> And He shall give you the desires of your heart.
> —PSALM 37:3–4

Legacy is not for those with a selfish, superficial, short-term mindset. A negative or narrow mind cannot even begin to see a legacy, let alone set one in motion! Legacy requires faith, imagination, passion, and compassion. Legacy is for those who decide to be the strongest link possible to the lineage God has placed them in.

Legacy is our link not only to our possibilities but also to our responsibilities. We need to be aware of the life span of our deeds. The life span of our deeds will outlive us. Our attitudes and actions are linked from one generation to the next.

Don't be drawn into a life of pointless activity, which is possibly one of the more destructive forms of sin. Moving absently through daily routines with no connection to destiny is tragic. After all, what do you think grieves God? Is it our self-imposed religious rules, habits, and activities—"Do not touch, do not taste, do not handle" (Col. 2:21)? Or is it the preponderance of daily activities that lack an eternal connection?

I want to encourage you to add legacy to your daily routine. It will give you new insight into the importance of the little things you do, and it will help you understand your role to the ongoing purpose of God.

Remember the woman with the alabaster box? She had an eternal perspective. It took just a few moments, but her action had such an impact that Jesus said her story would be told wherever the gospel is preached! "What this woman has done will also be told as a memorial to her" (Matt. 26:13).

IS "DASH" ALL THERE IS?

When I see a grave marker with the name of a person and that little dash between their dates of birth and death, it makes me ponder life's meaning.

Were their lives just dashes through seamless and dreamless seasons? Were their desires dashed against the walls of disappointment and difficulties? Did they ever achieve the success they wanted? Did their lives reflect significance?

More importantly, what of your life? Will you get down to business—not busyness—before the number is added on the right side of the dash?

My ADD, which I consider an "add-on feature" of my brain, means I can do two or three things at the same time. Actually, I *have* to be doing two or three things, although I find it challenging to finish any of them.

As a result, I have spent a lot of time lost on the freeways of Southern California, drifting into some other world while engaged in the safety of my driving—but too bored to be watching for the proper exits. I now have a navigation system in my car that keeps me from getting lost half the time. I still manage to get distracted, and when I do, I hear an annoying voice telling me to make a U-turn. I have missed my exit yet again.

When you're driving on a twelve-lane freeway at, let's say, fifty-five-ish miles an hour, it is not possible to turn around. But within a minute or so, the system will find me in my wandering way and reroute my path to get me where I need to go.

Thank God the Holy Spirit will always reroute me when I get off course. He will find me wherever I've drifted off to and make a way to get me to my destiny.

We all have an "eternal navigation system" that will lead us to our destiny. It could represent another acronym for DNA—our "**D**ivine **N**avigation **A**ctivator" system.

The wisdom of the ages is flowing through your veins. Listen. Learn.

The amazing thing is that when we don't listen, God takes our mistakes and makes such good use of them that you would think they were in the original plan. So perfect are His ways that our sinful or stupid ways (sometimes both) can be turned into something good for His purpose.

Our *mess-age* becomes a powerful *message* to our descendants.

Are you aware of how much impact you have on your DNA?

Have you gone through a tragedy when everything in you told you to quit but you didn't? How about when you were faced with a temptation and you resisted? Do you remember the day you shut down your computer and changed your password so as to not continue on the destructive path you were on? Have you confessed to a friend that you were struggling in your marriage and needed accountability to stop the flirtation that had begun with a co-worker? What about the day you chose to bless rather than curse the inconsiderate driver who pulled out in front of you on the highway (causing the latte stain on your freshly dry-cleaned clothes)?

Your grandchildren will face similar situations. Will the virtue and strength you contributed to their DNA help them to resist also?

There is a code that will provide guidance for you. Follow that coded instinct, and you will enter into a life that will allow you to achieve what you have always imaGENEd! Reach deep down within; draw from the bloodline that takes your lineage to another level.

Running the Race of Your Life

"So what does it take to be a successful pastor of a thriving ministry?"

A young pastor asked this question during a round of golf with a foursome of pastors. Two of them were pastors of very large churches. I happened to be one of the other two. No matter what our life's work may be, we all seek to learn how to improve and go to the next level. This would be an opportunity for me to gain insight and ideas.

The first pastor responded with an intimidating summary of his weekly schedule. "Well, Monday and Tuesday are usually spent traveling to my many speaking engagements. On Wednesday I have my staff meeting with our current staff of thirty. Our packed-out midweek service is on Thursday. Every Friday I devote time to writing. My seventh book will be published next month. Saturday I prepare for multiple Sunday services. We had over ten thousand people at our services last week!"

With just a slight variation, the other pastor described his week. Then the young pastor turned to me and asked, "How about you? How do you spend your week?"

I couldn't compete with their achievements, so I chose a path of candor and comedy. "On Monday I usually quit! On Tuesday I realize that I don't know what else to do for a living. On Wednesday I preach to a half-empty auditorium. On Thursday I'm disappointed that more people didn't show up. On Friday I start preparing for the Word that will spark a move of God to propel my church into an unbelievable growth spurt. By Saturday I'm on fire. On Sunday I preach my heart out. On Monday I quit."

I tell this story with a bit of exaggeration, but that is typical when we feel discouraged. My fellow pastors were not trying to intimidate me, but I certainly was allowing myself to be intimidated.

Think of a time when you felt down and out. You know what I'm talking about. Think of one of those rainy days when you lost your feeling of purpose and were convinced that nothing you have ever done or ever will do could possibly matter. If life is a race, why try? You are so far behind that others have lapped you, and you are simply not going to win this race.

It happens to us all in our roles as parents, in our careers, even in our relationship with God. We become overwhelmed with our under-achievement. Life feels like a rat race, and the rats are winning! Maybe we've entered the wrong race. We did not sign up for a sprint. It's time to pull out of this maddening race that's running us rather than being run by us.

You could call your life a *gen-e-RACE-tional* relay race. When you've run your laps, you will pass the baton to the next in your lineage. Every lap you run with integrity and intensity will help those who begin where you end. You will come to discover that running this race is not just about winning but about finishing your leg of the race.

The revelation of legacy has not only kept me in the game, but it has also given me a passion for the bigger prize. The prize is not just about me; its not just about now. It's not just personal but generational, and with eternal consequences, too.

With a generational view, I am able to remove the temporary and trivial perspective from my trials and tests. This allows me to see further down the road and absorb the bumps that would normally take me out of the race.

Running a legacy is not a sprint. We are engaged in a marathon. It is a race that will still be going on long after we have passed from this life. We will see the finish line from the grandstand of heaven.

What we believe and what we are willing to believe God for is only as effective as our willingness to stay with it. Our confidence stands on the promise that what we are investing our lives in will be watched over and completed by Him who has begun the work.

The plans God has for you are so big, so meaningful, and so important that it will take both you and the generations to come to comprehend and complete the work. Don't let pride cause you to think that your own will is the most important part of your destiny. Your life is part of a plan that isn't being made up as you go. You are important enough to require some planning that can be traced to past generations.

God transcends time; He sees all things from beginning to end. The reality of your legacy is an irreversible certainty. It is solid as rock, unmovable, enduring, and everlasting. However, you can delay the purpose of God with short-term or superficial attitudes. Time is not an issue for God, but it may be for you!

Hooked by a Book: Why I Had to Write This Book

When the concept of writing this book on legacy initially came to me, I considered giving the concept away to one of my friends who could reach more people with the message.

"Dad! Don't do it," was the adamant response of my daughter, Kara. My wife, Jeannie, had already weighed in with her opinion. I knew she wanted me to write this book.

"What does it matter whether or not I write the book? Who cares who gets the credit?" I said, feeling almost humble.

"Because," Kara insisted, "I have books inside of me. Unless you open that door, I'll never have an opportunity!"

Bam!

How selfish of me! This project is not just about me!

I was hiding from a message that God has given me and is going to hold me accountable for. The point is not whether the book inside of me ended up in your hands or at a closeout sale at the back of a bookstore.

This is my mandate. If the act of obedience is only the seed of what could be, then so be it!

This is exactly what each of you will discover when you are challenged to step up to your calling. You must live your life totally extended, hopelessly abandoned, passionately pursuing every opportunity and door God makes available.

The Three Most Important Questions

You may be feeling a little intimidated right now. Why do you need a legacy? All this talk about multigenerational responsibility and eternal accountability feels like a lot of pressure.

Every moment of your life matters!

You may be thinking, "Why can't I just enjoy my life? Maybe when I get older I'll focus on this legacy stuff. Right now, I have too many activities."

I'm not trying to add to your overtasked, overbooked, overworked life. Just the opposite. My objective is to give you a renewed perception and hope to believe that the little things you do in your daily life can actually be a link to the ongoing purpose of God. No wasted moments.

Benjamin Franklin is credited with creating three critical questions each of us must answer:

- Where did you come from?

- Where are you going?

- To whom are you accountable?

Many years before, Paul answered these very questions in Acts 17: "He has made *from one blood*...and has determined...*the boundaries of their dwellings*....in Him we live and move and have our being....He has *appointed a day* on which He will judge the world" (Acts 17:26–28, 31, emphasis added).

The three answers are:

- Where did you come from? From a specific determined bloodline.

- Where are you going? Toward a life of purpose found "in Him."

- To whom are you accountable? To God on the Day of Judgment.

These three questions may be the most important ones you'll ever answer.

Answer them well!

CHAPTER 4

Building an Enduring Household

Will your house rock or roll?

Believe on the Lord Jesus Christ, and you will be saved, you and your household.

—ACTS 16:31

IF YOU ARE GOING TO TRAVEL ON THIS ADVENTURE OF LEGACY, YOU will need faith. Faith is your visa to the land of legacy. A godly legacy requires faith. What is faith? How does it work? How do you know you have it?

- Faith gives you the *expectation* and courage to dream and to live up to the disciplines of that dream.

- Faith *expresses* itself with works and is not just a passing thought.

- Faith *endures* through the testing that will inevitably come.

- Faith that is based upon the Word of God can be *explained* with conviction.

- Faith *expands* each time it is practiced. Faith can begin small, like a mustard seed, and become the huge tree under which birds gather.

You'd think that the miraculous results of a walk of faith would attract a huge following. Not so! Many people shun a life of faith. It is simply too risky!

Most of us prefer a more logical and reasonable lifestyle with its predictability and control rather than the adventure of faith. We allow security and stability to lock up our dreams and hold them captive. The mundane lures us in, and we view the call of faith as a threat to our (actually) boring life.

The faith walk is a threat to our feelings. We need to realize that feelings and faith are not the best traveling companions. Which of the two will you choose to lead your life?

We love to tell the stories of the Bible—David and Goliath, Joshua and the crumbling walls of Jericho, and the three Hebrew boys whom God brought through the fiery furnace. We rejoice in the God who always comes through, overcoming the improbable to accomplish the impossible. But put us in that same setting? We panic at the very idea of having nothing but a slingshot to face our giants. We certainly would never allow ourselves to go into battle with nothing but a trumpet in our hands.

Walk into a fiery furnace? Please!

And we wonder, "Where is the God of miracles today?"

He stands in the shadows of the giants and walls that you keep avoiding.

He is in the fiery furnace that melted your confidence before it was turned up seven times hotter. Why, it was just getting interesting when you bailed.

When will you dare to live a life that at least occasionally puts your faith on the spot? God is waiting for you to step into that spot.

When will your faith become something that is desired and not dreaded?

When will you begin to set a faithful and courageous example for those who follow you—your children, your church, or the entrepreneurs and leaders of the next generation?

Without faith, there is no legacy. The very idea of a legacy is based on the intangible belief that what you do matters, that your actions will be transferred into some form of influence beyond your life. That, my friend, takes faith!

What is faith? What does it look like? How do you recognize it when you see it? Faith is something that cannot be seen by the natural eye.

Whatever can be viewed or completely understood by our mind is not faith. Faith always transcends our "sight and sound" logic. "While we do not look at the things which are seen, but at the things which are not seen. For the things which are seen are temporary, but the things which are not seen are eternal" (2 Cor. 4:18).

So how can we know when we are living in faith, acting from faith, or building a legacy on faith? How can we spot the real deal?

THE FOURFOLD FORCE OF FAITH

The Greek version of the Bible is far more expressive than the English version. In Greek, there are many different words for *faith*. Each word reveals a different facet of the whole meaning of the word. I want to focus on the following four facets—*truth*, *action*, *commitment*, and *supernatural force*.

Your legacy built on faith can be pictured as a three-legged stool. The top of the stool is the base of truth, which represents your belief system. The three legs that hold up those beliefs are the actions that express your belief, the commitment to stick to your belief, and the supernatural force that you are counting on to see what you believe come to pass.

What do you believe? How do your actions demonstrate what you believe (and where is there a discrepancy)? How have you signaled your commitment to what you believe? What methods do you use to invite the supernatural force into your faith? To build a successful legacy, each of these four facets of faith must be involved.

CAN YOU BELIEVE IT?

Your beliefs form a body or system of truth. Your belief system determines your values and is the basis of the choices you make as you live your life. What do you believe so deeply and thoroughly that you would stake your life on it?

Some people's only conviction is that they don't believe anything with conviction. Others attempt to build a life upon the shifting sand of current ideology or the favorite philosophy of the year.

Martin Luther King Jr. said, "A man who won't die for something is not fit to live." Commitment validates what we say we believe. Legacy requires a solid base of commitment to build upon.

A man was struggling with the phone directory inside a phone booth (remember those?), trying to get it outside into the light so he could read it. A little boy walked by and said helpfully, "Sir, if you'll get in all the way and shut the door, a light will come on!"

Get in all the way! When we make the commitment and "get in" to what we believe, and also shut the door on any doubt or hesitation, the *light* comes on!

Until you invest energy and thought into defining your belief system, you are in danger of making choices that will have consequences that restrict or impair the possibilities of your legacy. If you wait too long to commit to a foundation of faith in something, you may limit what the next generation has available to build upon.

All legacies begin on the foundation of faith. A dream is birthed by faith in the promise and the possibility of this statement: "Believe and you shall receive." A dream, when faithfully followed, becomes a legacy. Become fatalistically faithful.

The approximate eighteen inches between your mind (intelligence) and your heart (intuition) can seem like a million miles when you haven't integrated the two into a system of beliefs that guide and govern your life. Make the link; connect the chain of faith to your legacy.

I dare you to believe that your life is a God-given gift that has possibilities and responsibilities from and to God. A life that carries equity is priceless. You are eighteen inches from that legacy. Think about it.

Your life is like a building towering toward the heavenly purpose of God. One floor upon another, one dream upon another, generation upon generation, the plans of the kingdom are established. "According to the grace of God which was given to me, as a wise master builder I have laid the foundation, and another builds on it. But...take heed how he builds on it" (1 Cor. 3:10).

I love the way God had the prophets of old write Scripture in such a way that the good, the bad, and too often the ugly are exposed. Reading the stories of some of the great men of the Bible gives us hope that God can use us—even with our baggage and blunders. For example, King David was called a man after God's own heart (Acts 13:22). Yet he was told that he would not be allowed to build the house of the Lord. Because of the innocent blood that was shed through decisions that were made in haste and haughty disobedience to God, David would be denied that privilege. But God did promise David that his seed would fulfill the dream.

David did everything he could to prepare his son Solomon for the achievement. David had literally billions of dollars in today's currency laid aside for the building of a temple that he would never see. David's attitude was: "I may not be able to do the actual building, but I will arrange my influence and affluence so that my son will succeed."

> When your days are fulfilled and you rest with your fathers, I will set up your seed after you, who will come from your body, and I will establish his kingdom.
>
> —2 Samuel 7:12

> Now it was in the heart of my father David to build a temple for the name of the Lord God of Israel. But the Lord said to my father David, "Whereas it was in your heart to build a temple for My name, you did well that it was in your heart. Nevertheless you shall not build the temple, but your son who will come from your body, he shall build the temple for My name."
>
> —1 Kings 8:17–19

And build a temple Solomon did. The temple was like no other. There had never been nor will there ever be one more glorious. (See 1 Kings 10.)

Without a view from above and a perception from eternity, we will find it easy to quit. When we fail, we can be tempted to make it final. Legacy becomes the lens of faith. From that perspective we see that *every decision matters!*

When traveling to Europe, I'm so impressed with the magnificent churches. The carefully carved wood and enormous ceilings with their detailed paintings show the sacrifice and painstaking efforts the people put forth.

What really staggers my mind is how long it took to build them. The chapel of Florence, Italy, took over five hundred years to build. Over ten generations were willing to give, work, and support a building that most of them would never see or attend services in. Instant gratification was not in their agenda. They were willing to build for generations to come for a cause that was beyond the "me" and "now."

That's the kind of heart it takes to build legacy.

Your actions confirm or deny what you believe. They determine how your beliefs make a difference in your life or how they don't really affect it at all. Many people say they believe something but lack the faith to live a life that expresses that belief.

The narrow passage one must walk to enter the door of His truth requires focus and fervency, but the rewards are eternal.

Will you live a life that never breaks out of the confines of comfortable living? Will you let fear hold you back from even trying? Jesus told the parable of the talents. The disappointment was not over the servant trying and failing but for failing to even try! The parable of the talents implies we will not be held accountable for what we failed at but at what we failed to attempt. (See Matthew 24.)

My friend Greg Albertyn grew up with the dream of becoming a motocross racer. Everything he did was focused on that goal.

Then, when he was twelve years old, his mom got a "word of the Lord" that he would become the world champion of motocross. Greg says, "Receiving this type of word sets you up for a season of testing. God births a dream in you, but you have to have staying power. You need to stand on the Word and keep going until you break through to the next realm."

He moved from his homeland of South Africa to Europe by himself at the age of seventeen in order to compete. He went through two years of injury after injury. It just made him work harder than ever. His efforts rewarded him with three world championships, but the "big one," the U.S. championship, seemed to be slipping out of reach. Age and injuries were mounting against his dream.

I remember the conversation I had with him during that time. I wish

I could say that I gave him a great "never give up" speech, but I too thought that the end had come to his career.

Finally, he decided that even though he knew God had called him to this dream, unless he had a major breakthrough he was quitting. He got on his knees and prayed, "I am serious. I am ready to quit." But like all champions, he found the courage to persevere.

The next day he won both races, and later that year he would go on to win the U.S. National Championship. Today as a husband, father, and successful businessman, he continues to live a life that expresses his beliefs.

Your commitment to your beliefs demonstrates your faithfulness. Faith expressed with fidelity and endurance over time becomes faithfulness. Significant faithfulness is a requirement of legacy building.

Your faith is the foundation that others will build upon. Your faithfulness to your dreams, relationships, and covenants determines how solid the foundation is for the next generation.

Extend, expand, and put an expectation on your faith in a way that requires God to step in so you won't look like a fool.

HOOK, LINE, AND THINKER

There's a thin line between a man fishing and a man standing on a riverbank, holding a pole and looking like an idiot. A very thin line.

In our lives, faith is that thin line. Very few will see it besides you and God. God has given you that faith—a measure of faith that connects you to overflowing blessings (Rom. 12:3). Do you live with that *tug* of faith pulling on your heart? Are you staring at the possibilities, or are you striving for them as if your life depends on it?

The fish—your provisions—are not going to just jump into your boat! You will have to cast your line of faith and catch what God has ready and waiting for those who dare to believe!

What do you believe in? What will you believe for? How long will you stand in faith for what you believe in and for? In Hebrews 6:12, we are advised: "That you do not become sluggish, but imitate those who through faith and patience inherit the promises."

Today, grant yourself permission to envision what could be. Don't worry if you can't accomplish the task. Just take the first step, and begin to see the vision.

I have opportunities to minister in other countries, and recently I went to Venezuela. Pastor Javier heads the church that hosted a training conference for EQUIP, John Maxwell's effective ministry. The people of Venezuela are very poor, despite the fact that the country is the third largest oil source in the world, and Pastor Javier was raised in a very poor family.

He started his church with eight people, and it soon grew to over fifteen hundred. The congregation lacked financial resources, so it didn't seem as if they would ever be able to buy property. Pastor Javier began to pray for a way to finance his work in the kingdom.

He was led to search the papers one day, and he noticed that a major airline was selling a fleet of airplanes. Without any money, he bid on them. With only twenty thousand dollars in the bank, he also bid on an eight-million-dollar property for a church! His offers were accepted on both bids.

Miraculously, someone in the United States leased the planes and paid three years in advance. Now, many clients, including leaders in the Christian community who minister in his country, charter the planes.

The church is one of the most influential congregations in that country. It's a church where nearly ten thousand people gather weekly for worship. If you were to visit, there are two things that you would see: a church that prays with a passion like nothing I have ever seen, and a vast amount of youth and young couples that make up the majority of the congregation.

I traveled to Venezuela with Rudy (the Los Angeles fireman I introduced to you in chapter 1). At the time, our church was in the middle of a campaign to raise capital for our own land and building. After Rudy heard Pastor Javier's testimony, he said to me with fire in his eyes, "Pastor, we are thinking too small!" We both realized that God could do more than we ask or even imagine.

Are you limiting God? Is what you are doing big enough for God to build a lasting legacy? If you alone can accomplish your desires, if in your lifetime alone you can achieve your dreams, I am certain it's not a legacy. Go back to the drawing table and enlarge your vision.

Now to Him who is able to do exceedingly abundantly above all
that we ask or think, according to the power that works in us.
—Ephesians 3:20

Timing Is Everything

The Bible tells many stories of those who received a supernatural faith
from God for a specific time and purpose.

Esther was a young orphan girl whose parents were killed by a
wicked king. She was raised by her cousin and lived under constant
oppression. How likely was it that she would be chosen from thousands to be the wife of the king? It was unthinkable that a Jewish girl
could become a queen to a Gentile nation. Being forced by orders to
prepare for her one night with the king, she was pampered with exotic
baths and perfumes and cosmetics for twelve months as preparation
for her first date with him.

Did being "wined and dined" distract her from the purpose God
prepared and positioned her for? Absolutely not. With no regard to her
peril and the potential loss of all the power and pleasure she had come
to know, she said, "If I perish, I perish" (Esther 4:16).

With those words, she went before the king to save her people.
Perhaps the Jewish nation as we know it would have ceased to exist had
it not been for Esther. Mordecai's words spoken to Esther may ring true
for you today: "Who knows whether you have come to the kingdom
for such a time as this?" (v. 14). What about the trouble you've experienced? What about the pain you've endured? Everything in your life,
the struggles and the achievements, may have prepared you "for such
a time as this."

This is your time. Someday you will enter heaven to stand in awe
of the heroes of the faith. You might say, "Look, there's Abraham and
Moses and the mighty kings and prophets who subdued kingdoms and
saw God's glory! There's David the giant-killer, and look at those who
suffered violence and overcame persecution without whimpering or
whining. There's Esther, who attained a position of great favor so she
could save her people."

As you stand beside these great people of faith, you are going to want
to have done something worthwhile for God's kingdom.

Every one of those *heroes* was a *zero* at some point in his or her life. That ought to take the *test* out of our *testimony* and give us every reason to go for it.

God only measures our faith, not our failures. He forgets our failures but transfers every act of faith we perform. Often our biggest failure can be the greatest springboard for the purpose God has in mind for us.

Impossible Is Nothing for God

This chapter began by asking what faith looks like and how to know when it's the real deal. Would you believe me if I told you that there is a foolproof way to spot it, and it can be summed up in one word? That word is *impossible*!

Impossible! Now we're talking God's lingo. Now we are getting God stirred up. Our God is offended by a life that never reaches into the realm of impossibility, because the realm of impossibility is the realm of faith. Are you willing to go there?

Can you imagine believing in a cause so great that you could not live life without it?

Have you heard the voice, captured a view, or felt heaven's virtue bidding you to step out of your rut and follow the whisper of a daring dream from another world?

The biggest thing you could ever imagine happening in your life will fall short of what God wants to do and *will* do if you can see beyond the temporary to envision the eternal.

Live your life beyond belief. Believe in yourself as God believes in you. Believe that you can see your dreams come true. Dreams are not just luxuries for the elite while the rest of us drudge through life with pressures and problems too real to escape. Dreams are the solutions for man's pollutions! Once a dream grabs you by the heart, it becomes a call of God on your life to advance His purpose on the earth. Every dream is a legacy in the making.

God is attracted to the faith in that which seems impossible for man. Let me encourage you to have a faith so grand that you must trust God for any possible outcome. Combined with your faith and your faithfulness, God will release the supernatural faith that becomes the secret ingredient that transforms the impossible into the possible. I like adidas's slogan, "Impossible is nothing." That's the kind of mind-set we need to have. Slip into something uncomfortable for a change.

We will have plenty of time in heaven to be comfortable. Now is the time to step out of your safe and stodgy comfort zone for the sake of your legacy. Let your thinking be so big and beyond your own ability so that it will absolutely, positively, without any doubt whatsoever take God to make it happen. Dip into the paint of your imagination, and draw a picture that is so spectacular and meaningful that it could not possibly be fulfilled by yourself or in your lifetime. When it comes to faith, no reasonable offer will be accepted—only the unreasonable and humanly unachievable offer will God accept.

That's the language of legacy. That's the potential of faith.

You have within you a slingshot called faith, just as David had. Now put a stone of passion into the pocket and sling away toward your obstacle. A dream slays a giant every time! Give the future generations something to talk about. The fierce battles you've fought, the persistent obstacles

> **Every problem you overcome will matter!**

you've overcome, the painful process—all these difficulties become part of the drama that makes for inspiring legacy.

WILL YOUR HOUSE HOLD?

David was a legacy legend. Before he became king, he faced a terrible injustice, and as a result, he lost his temper. He could have lost more; he could have lost his legacy.

"You have every right to kill him! My husband is acting out what his name means—a fool," Abigail cried. "But God has sent me with a message for you. If you take vengeance on his unwarranted behavior, the plan that God has for you will be in jeopardy!"

Abigail had come to stop David from avenging the foolish behavior of her husband, Nabel. The message she gave him at the risk of her own life is the message we need to hear today when we too face injustice and indifference. "For the LORD will certainly make for my lord an enduring house, because my lord fights the battles of the LORD, and evil is not found in you throughout your days" (1 Sam. 25:28).

God had determined to build an "enduring house" using David and his bloodline. David was facing a defining moment in his life. He was coming to realize how much his life mattered—not just in a personal way but also in a generational way—and that his response would have eternal consequences.

The promised Messiah was to come from the lineage of David. David could not afford to allow a temporary problem, no matter how justified, to cost him his future. David responded right to the wrong done, reminding us that it's never right to be wrong.

Legacy endured!

We should not be paranoid and live intimidated over every possible misstep we take. At the same time, we should not be passive and slothful. We all face events in our lives that can provoke reactions of anger, revenge, and despair. Even when it may appear in the "temporal" moment to be justified, we must see through the "eternal eyes" of legacy.

Develop a *legacy consciousness* that will become a voice reminding you that someone in your lineage will be impacted by your attitudes and actions. A legacy-lived life adds up in value. You will experience a greater worth to everything about your life.

The foundation of your legacy is vital. The resources and relationships that you will be given are for you to build on the foundation for your "enduring house."

Every one of our reactions to life's problems matters!

I believe that Jesus was speaking of legacy when He told the parable of two men who each set out to build a house. One man built upon a rock. The other man built his house on the sand. Both used the same material, invested the same hard work, and perhaps even used the same blueprint. (See Matthew 7:24–27.)

"After the rains came"—this could represent the things that come down from above—things like God's instructions and rebuke, which can destroy our house like a storm if not built on the rock. Even the blessings that "come down" from God can result in "beating down" our house if we become ungrateful and indifferent. Gratitude is a foundational pillar in building our legacy.

"Then the floods rose"—this could represent the things that rise up from the enemy, such as attacks on your finances, family, or faith—evil and negative forces that attempt to wash your household away. "When the enemy comes in like a flood, the Spirit of the LORD will lift up a standard against him" (Isa. 59:19). Be certain of this: it won't be *if* but *when* the enemy comes. We have an enemy that seeks to devour our personal and generational potential. Your seed is the entire plan the enemy has to perpetuate his agenda. It's a fact that Satan has no reproducing ability. His agenda is only perpetuated through your household lineage. The watering and washing of your seed to a path channeled for his destructive plan is something we must contend with. Let the Spirit of the Lord raise up a standard for you.

"And the winds blew" are the things that come horizontally from man, such as verbal, emotional, or even physical abuse. The "winds" of man's doctrines and deceitful ways have destroyed as many legacies as the devil has.

There will be many opportunities to be offended and, as a result, cause your house to fall. It hurts when people, sometimes our friends or even family, say or do things that would tear us down. Pass on the opportunities for offense.

Only the man who built his house on the rock survived.

The rock to build our "enduring house" on is the truth of God's Word. Legacy must be built on the rock of truth.

Our opinions will wash away over time. The sands of shifting relativity that move and groove with the tide of opinions and trends will toss your legacy on the waves of disappointment.

Although it will take a lifetime to leave what you believe, you can start building your legacy today.

Commit to the legacy-driven life; use it as a blueprint to design your enduring house. Your house will stand for generations against all storms, floods, and winds.

> Whoever hears these sayings of Mine, and does them, I will liken him to a wise man who built his house on the rock: and the rain descended, the floods came, and the winds blew and beat on that

house; and it did not fall, for it was founded on the rock. Now everyone who hear these sayings of Mine, and does not do them, will be like a foolish man who built his house on the sand: and the rain descended, the floods came, and the winds blew and beat on that house; and it fell. And great was its fall.

—MATTHEW 7:24–27

PART TWO

Your Past

Your deeds affect your seeds. Your choice today becomes your voice tomorrow to the next generation.

CHAPTER 5

In Every Deed
There Is a Seed

You will live for generations to come

He is the faithful God who keeps his covenant for a thou-sand generations... on those who love him and obey his commands.

—DEUTERONOMY 7:9, NLT

"VANCIE, IS THAT YOU IN THERE?"

Many times when I look at Jeannie, I'll ask that question.

I never did get the privilege to meet my wife's mother. Vancie died of cancer at the age of forty-four. I met Jeannie six months after her mother's untimely death.

I am determined, however, to discover who and what she was like. Through what I call a "personality by deduction" theory, I have formed an opinion of who I think Vancie was. I observe Odie, who was her husband for twenty-five years, and then her children, and then deduct what I think is from Odie's side of the genes. Then I reason that Vancie is in the rest. Not very scientific, but it works for me.

I love to discover the Vancie who is being revealed to me through Jeannie a little more each day.

This is what I do know. Vancie loved the ministry. She taught her children to respect the ministry. She served the pastors and gave sacrificially even to the point of her doing without. Her love for music found expression only by insisting her children learn to play the piano. She dreamed, after helping to build a successful business with her husband, of traveling the world. Missionary work would have been her ultimate dream come true.

It never happened. Or did it?

All five of her children are musicians. As musicians, they have touched the world through travel, written a Grammy-nominated song, sent musical instruments to third world countries, and recorded songs that have been heard around the world. Lynn (who went to be with the Lord), Sharon, Theresa, and Nathan, who is also an ordained minister, along with Jeannie, have all exceeded their mother's dreams.

The lens of legacy gives us a view of our lives with a generational perspective. The distinction from one generation to the next is made known more by purpose than personality. God rewards and responds to the generational—not just the personal—responsibilities in our legacies. Your success is not personal as much as it is generational. Your legacy is not just in your deeds—it's in your seed!

A very revealing insight into why and how our lives are shaped is hinted at in John 9:1–2: "As Jesus passed by, He saw a man who was blind from birth. And His disciples asked Him, saying, 'Rabbi, who sinned, this man or his parents, that he was born blind?'" The limited knowledge of that time would not have allowed the people to be able to comprehend just what Christ was alluding to. That's not the case anymore!

I think I understand the context, and Jesus did answer them by saying that it was neither this man's fault nor his parents. Jesus would heal the man, and the real purpose would be made known. The miracle the blind man received would be to glorify God!

Every action and attitude matters.

But the question is still relevant to what we all are asking.

Why are we the way we are? Is it our *deed* or our *seed*?

It's fair to say that we are what we are by nature and nurture. As already discussed, we are not attempting to be scientists or to solve this often-heated debate, a debate that has been passed down from...

well…I've made my point. Although, I do think that it is beyond interesting that Jesus spat on the ground (clearly a sign of the influence of DNA) in order to heal the man's eyes. The dust and divine breath of God are still what make up man's DNA.

What I am declaring is that our actions do not just play out on the fields of sowing and reaping in our lifetime. Our actions are sown into the fertile ground of generations. In every deed there is a seed.

How your children react to the seeds of your deeds in them will be their choice. There will be no excuses accepted for any bad behavior. As I said before, there are only explanations.

The more you know about what kind of seed you have in you, the better you can understand how to resist and/or respond.

The biological factors of our existence are undeniable. It's not that complex. One mommy. One daddy. One precious life! The seed and the egg still make up the miraculous genesis of our lives. From that seed comes the destiny that will build a legacy.

How we view and value our family will add virtue to our legacy.

What is its worth? Who is responsible for maintaining that worth?

Family relationships are the center of our relational universe. If we are *off center* with our family and/or covenant relationships, everything will be out of orbit, out of order. It's a pity to observe those who think they live in their own little world, living as if they were dropped off the planet with no obligations to those from whom they came or to those who will follow. These are people who have the deceitful disease of "me." They are like the guy who said, "But enough about me. Let's talk about you; what do you think about me?"

The selfish gene is the most destructive gene in our family closets.

Everything about you does matter, and how you take that responsibility to heart for your seed will bring heightened awareness to your every deed. That's why the enemy strives and too often succeeds in the relentless pursuit to destroy families.

The law of relational gravity provides stability in our lives. It keeps us secured to the ground so we don't just float off into our own selfish inner space.

Relational gravity includes our biological and biblical families. Our biological family is established through our bloodline and DNA. Our biblical family is shaped through covenantal relationships, such as marriage, adoption, church, and even covenant business relationships. Just as our past relationships have influenced us, the newly formed or renewed relationships we make today will influence our seed.

Future generations of our children, church, and community relationships become part of our galaxy. Each of our plans align like planets in sync with one another. The decisions and direction that you choose today will affect a long lineage of lives for a very long time.

Our acts and behavior affect or infect the generations that follow us. We need to be constantly aware of the consequences of our deeds.

I want those of you who have no children to know clearly how vital the role of community and church relationships are to building legacy.

When I was sixteen years of age, I fought my demons of rebellion and the rejection of my parent's faith. Two people saved me from a sure path of destruction—Lou Beko and Kathy Palmer. Neither of them married or had any biological children. Their passion for Christ and the dedicated love shown to me during that time will only be able to be measured in eternity.

Whatever legacy I have will carry the DNA of what they helped put in me during that critical time of my life. I say that to encourage you who are not married or do not have biological children—your role in building a legacy is not diminished. Through covenant relationships you can be "grafted" into multiple legacies that will have eternal consequences.

This is why the apostle Paul carried so much influence. He saw young men like Timothy as his *sons* of the faith.

From a "No Name" to a "Know Name"

If there is a line to stand behind in order to have a legacy, then the legend I was honored to interview on national television started his life at the back of that line. In 1912, having a child out of wedlock was unacceptable in society, but nevertheless a newborn little baby boy just a few hours old was dropped off at the local hospital.

A mistake?

There was no note and no sign of who his parents were or where he came from. He was just left—the boy with no name. A Baptist preacher and his wife decided to adopt him. Even though they were over fifty years of age, they knew they had to take this little boy as their own. By being "grafted" in a godly legacy, he would discover the personal benefits and passion of having a new bloodline that would fuse his biological and adoptive heritage with surprising success.

With a strong spiritual foundation and a drive for adventure, this young man became one of the biggest names in television history. Who is the "no-name" boy? Art Linkletter.

Art and I sat at a local deli for nearly three hours one day as he told me many of his fascinating stories. I could not help but see the obvious links between both sides of his lineage.

For example, Art, who was the originator of what we now call "reality" TV, discovered this unique approach by "mistake"—what would appear to be a fluke. Someone asked him if he would be willing to do a radio show. He agreed, and his first show was to cover a press conference of sorts with President Franklin Roosevelt as the president arrived off a ship at the San Diego port.

With microphone in hand and a live audience waiting all over the San Diego airwaves, he scrambled to fill the airwaves as the delay of the president's appearance lingered on. With brilliant reaction he began to talk to people walking among the huge gathering. The comments were funny, enlightening, and spontaneous.

On that day the popular "man on the street" interview concept was birthed. A young man left alone with a microphone turned this obstacle into an opportunity, and the rest, as they say, is history. Today, not only does Art have a biological legacy, but his influence on television and broadcasting is felt in some shape or form every day around the world.

The no-name child became the most known name in media history. Legacy can begin under all conditions and circumstances. What's your story? How will you take your life and use it to start or sustain a godly legacy?

Everyone has a link to legacy. The chain of events and experiences of your life form a lineage that ties every action and attitude to your legacy.

Your legacy is transferred through the undeniable principle that will change the way you think about your life forever—*in every deed there is a seed.*

Your family is a branch, a DNA extension of the human family tree. The *characteristics*, *charisma*, and *chaos* of our lives are greatly influenced by the deeds done from whom our seed has come.

The virtues you form, the gifting you develop, the problems you solve in your personal life will become invaluable to your seed.

These truths have long been recognized in Scripture. (See Exodus 20:5–6; Deuteronomy 7:9.) The connection between the actions of one generation and the next was common knowledge in ancient culture. From land, possessions, and debt to family favors and feuds, all were passed down from one generation to the next.

> **Be aware and beware of the deeds you are sowing to and in your seed.**

The infamous feud in American folklore between the Hatfields and the McCoys, which began when Floyd Hatfield stole a hog from Randolph McCoy in 1878, shows that the grudges and unresolved issues of our parents can be carried on by future generations. More than twelve people were killed in this perpetuated feud.

A tragic occurrence in modern cultures' tendencies, especially in the West, is to promote the individual life over the community life. The mantras for our society are: "To each his own," "Travel your own path," and "Do your own thing." This has led us to believe that we live lives unto ourselves with no accountability to our past or future. This individualism has made community life merely that which is to be tolerated rather than celebrated.

The discoveries of how much influence our blood carries should cause us to reevaluate the significance of our heritage. Family is more than having the same last name. It's more than living in the same environment.

Our lives are a reflection—quite literally—of the deeds of our forefathers. No act done, no attitude dwelt upon, no achievement delighted in will stand alone. It will be passed down to your seed. Parents, church members, teachers, community leaders, all of us have the "deed-to-seed" connection, which is transferred to the next generation.

I saw this in my parents' lives. They took plenty of heat for performing dramas in the church, including the bringing of animals into the sanctuary for theatrical purposes. Years later, their children have gone on to develop several innovative ideas that have impacted many churches around the world. My sister and her husband, Sheila and Kevin Gerald, pastor Champions Centre in Tacoma, Washington. Their church is one of the largest in the Northwest. They produce some of the greatest Christmas and Easter dramas in the Northwest.

My brother Joe is an executive with a major company in California and has also produced plays in many cities throughout America. My other brother Steve has created Bible-based productions that have filled churches all over the country. With a cast of a thousand people and live animals of all sorts, including horses and camels, the indoor set he has built includes an indoor replica of Jerusalem and of Calvary, complete with fire and rain.

Steve and his wife, Melody, pastor Family Christian Center in Munster, Indiana—the same church my parents founded fifty years ago. Today this megachurch is one of the most influential churches in America. They are also known for their spectacular dramas.

My parents never saw their church grow past five hundred people. Yet, the ministries of all of their children combined touch the lives of tens of thousands weekly through our churches and media programs.

The small beginnings of their efforts have flourished into a harvest of influence. I'm sure my parents did not understand fifty years ago that their "out-of-the-box" thinking would spark fresh, creative ideas that would be implemented in many churches. They certainly did not have the knowledge we have today to grasp the transferable potential of their actions.

By the way, they are still at it. Rather than retiring, they started a powerful ministry that uses Christian principles to train young people for leadership in Sophia, Bulgaria. A couple years ago, Jeannie and I took our kids (including Doug, our son-in-law) to see the ongoing legacy of their grandparents. They are seventy-six years of age and still "accumulating" a spiritual equity line for their seed.

What are you doing today toward your generational harvest through the sacrificial seeds of your actions? Your blood is ready to carry your deeds to the next generation.

Times, Tribe, and Territory: Your Encoded Destiny

And He has made from one blood every nation of men to dwell on all the face of the earth, and has determined their preappointed times and the boundaries of their dwellings.

—Acts 17:26

This scripture can answer many of our questions and provide information needed in understanding the intent of God for all of mankind. I don't think there is a more key understanding of our life's purpose than what this verse declares.

Your destiny is in your DNA. To look closely at when, by whom, and where you were born is to be postured to discover and develop your destiny.

The word generation shares the same root with *genes, genesis, genealogy,* and *nation*. In the Bible, the word *generation* refers to these three areas, which I categorize as the *times, tribe,* and *territory* of our destiny.

Just as the order of the universe was set in motion, so it was with our lives. God set in motion the times (when we were born), tribes (by whom we were born), and the territory (where we were born), so that His determined purpose would be fulfilled.

It is no mistake that you came into this world, nor when you came and where you came from. God executes His plan for our life using all three.

Time: it's a *when-win*

Consider one of the great Old Testament leaders, Moses. Did it matter when he was born? Would his leadership have mattered a generation before?

Every single thing that God has planned for your life is attached to a particular point in time. If you study the prophetic passages of the Old Testament, you will become convinced of the impeccable timing of God's dealings throughout history.

The capture, captivity, and exodus of the children of Israel were predicted to the very year. (See Jeremiah 29:10.) The purpose of God has everything to do with timing. Moses could not have been born at any other time and do what he did in history. Fulfilling his destiny would require perfect timing. That means, among other things, the timing of his parents' meeting and having children. God oversaw the "when" of the purpose for Moses's life.

My daughter, Kara, and her husband, Doug, have had several miscarriages. These are painful events. With a miscarriage come so many questions and struggles of guilt, blame, and even a temptation to feel shame. In an attempt to bring comfort, I spoke to Kara about the whole timing issue.

"Your child must not come before its time. Just like you and Doug had to be born at the right time in order for the two of you to meet and become married, so your child (our grandchild) will need to make his or her grand entrance at the exact determined time of destiny." I believe destiny is that deliberate.

Your destiny and legacy are a "when-win" situation. Our role is to walk in obedience and be open to the bigger plan that may not always fit in our schedules. Moses could not have been born in another place or time. We may never know what his parents went through as they viewed the process through a glass darkly (1 Cor. 13:12), but legacy had it perfectly timed.

A woman was driving home one night, feeling very depressed and like she had never really belonged or mattered to anyone. She had been adopted at birth and was told that her birth mother returned to another country as soon as the adoption was concluded. She had tried to find her several times but always ran into resistance or dead ends.

As she was about to open the garage door that night, her husband called and told her to hurry because there was a very important phone call that she needed to take. When she got into the house, he said it was her mom. She looked at him and said, "Did someone die?"

"No," he said, "it's your *birth* mother."

Her birth mother found her after many long years. Her thoughts that very day remind us that God has set all things according to *His* timing.

God set the time of your birth. *When you came to Earth is as critical as that you came.* Think of the field of science. Every innovation of a great mind is built on the shoulders of those who went before them. Could there have been television before radio? Could there have been space rockets before airplanes?

Would Bill Gates or Oprah or Bono have had the same success at any other time in history?

Think about the leaders in the Christian community—their gifts match the moment. Who they have become has everything to do with when they came. It's a when-win situation.

Would your gifts and talents work in another time or place?

...for such a time as this.

—ESTHER 4:14

...as by one born out of due time.

—1 CORINTHIANS 15:8

Tribe: the great stock exchange

What good is the plan God has for you if you don't have the "goods" to accomplish it? Your DNA carries the character and charisma to accomplish your destiny. Study and understand your heritage, and you will more clearly see your legacy. We have all been given the right stuff to fulfill our destiny. One of the meanings for *generation* is "stock"— the stored up inventory from our tribe. God knew what we would need in our stock, or DNA, to be qualified for His purpose for our lives.

God works through tribes. Moses was removed from his natural family, but there came a day when it was in his destiny to reject their ways and step into the destiny in his DNA.

The more you understand where you came from, the more you will understand where you are going.

Territory: wherehouse of destiny

The place of our birth is part of our destiny. Moses was born an Israelite yet raised in an Egyptian home. The leadership skills he learned in the territory where he was raised played a major role in the fulfillment of his destiny.

The territory was as important as the timing and tribe. In the Book of Revelation, God refers to churches by the city in which they were located. The very location of the church determined the duties they were to perform. Each church had specific tasks to achieve and problems to solve. This tells me that there is a geographic connection to God's eternal plan. God placed you right where you are. God knows your address. He set the boundaries of your territory.

If God has predetermined my tribe, territory, and time, I want to know what He expects of me in response to His strategic plan for my life. The more we are aware of and align our lives to that eternal plan, the more value and victory our lives will have.

We may not be able to comprehend the magnitude of God's process, but we can cooperate in His master plan. The purpose of God is tracked in our bloodline. God makes no mistakes in determining the times and tribe and territory that we come through.

It's like a universal mosaic connected through time, and your life represents that one piece. You matter!

You don't come *from* your parents; you come *through* your parents. (See Jeremiah 1:5; John 1:13.)

If you have ever flipped through the television and caught James Robison on *LIFE Today*, you are seeing one of the great ministers of our day. He has preached as an evangelist for many years and is now feeding children around the world. He is definitely not a mistake. Yet he was conceived as a result of rape. *How* he came did not appear positive, but *that* he came has literally changed the lives of millions of people.

THE SCARLET THREAD

Another Bible story that shows how to convert lineage into legacy and demonstrates the link between DNA and destiny—long before science had a clue—is found in Joshua chapter 2.

A woman named Rahab, who came from a long lineage of what we would call a dysfunctional family, was raised as a Canaanite. Sexual perversion was not only a way of life in her world—it was a religion.

As a little girl, Rahab probably watched men come in and out of her house for the specific purpose of immoral activity. Her mother and her mother's mother were both prostitutes. Perhaps she vowed never to live that kind of life, much less subject her children to the environment she herself endured as a child.

However, like most women in her culture, Rahab fell into the same pattern of the women who came before her. Unfortunately, it was very easy for her to follow that same path.

Despite her good intentions, the expected fulfilled the expectation.

It seems unfair to be born into a family with a legacy far different from what you would choose. The laws of nature are not always to our liking. The same law that brings roses from a rose seed brings poison ivy from a poison ivy seed.

The good news is that God has made a way to reverse the curse.

Somehow, Rahab heard about the nation of Israel and that God's blessings were upon it. While spying out the land, two men from the camp of the Israelites entered her home to avoid capture by the guards of the city of Jericho. When the authorities knocked on her door and asked, "Have you seen these men?" she cleverly said, "No, I haven't."

When the men thanked her for saving their lives, Rahab said, "Thank me? I'll tell you how you can thank me. I want out of this pit I'm in. I didn't ask for this. I want a fair chance. I want a new life. I want redemption. I want what you people have. You have God. You have God's favor. I want in on that." (See Joshua 2:9–13.)

The men made a pledge and told her, "You take this scarlet thread and tie it to the roof of your house. When destruction comes on this city, God will spare your home with the scarlet thread." (See verse 18.)

The scarlet thread was a *symbol* of protection. Is it a coincidence that the thread was scarlet, the color of blood? Or is this a hint that the bloodline can convert one from destruction to destiny?

When the walls of Jericho came tumbling down, Rahab cowered under the table with her children and waited for her own walls to crumble. They did not. She probably grabbed her kids and cried out, "Let's get out of here! We've got a chance right now to bust out of this life of sin and strife."

The amazing part of the story is not that she and her family escaped without harm and survived the war. As we noted in chapter 1, the Gospel of Matthew provides the genealogy of Jesus. All the greats are listed: Abraham, Isaac, Jacob...right on down to Matthew 1:5, where we find *Rahab*!

Rahab became part of the GENEology of Jesus Christ. The same link that carried the iniquity of sin from one generation to the next was used to cross a bloodline of iniquity with a bloodline of equity that became the lineage of Christ.

Rahab chose to reverse her bloodline by choosing to walk in obedience to the favor of the God of Israel. In the process, she set in motion a new lineage. Rahab stepped out of her past lineage and stepped into the lineage of Jesus Christ.

How about you? You don't have to subject your life's future to the damage and destructiveness of the past. Stand up in faith and say, "This negative multigenerational pattern ends right here. I'm holding out for a new bloodline."

Rahab went from victim to victor.

As a pastor, I have no greater joy than watching people who have been victimized by the choices made in their lineage become victors by the blood of Christ. I have seen those who come from a past of poverty, drug abuse, infidelity, and the tragic event of divorce become the start of a new heritage.

CHANGE HAPPENS

Henry is the son of an immigrant worker who came to the United States from Mexico at the age of ten. By his late teens he was dealing drugs, including cocaine. He met Rosie, and they quickly moved in together. Rosie was raised a Christian but had become a prodigal of her faith. The power of the gospel caused her to be convicted of her own drug use. She would sometimes even talk to Henry about God and tell him, "We don't need to be doing this."

No one comes into this world without coming through the seed of a lineage. Your lineage is both your privilege and your responsibility.

Henry was listening. At the end of 1985 he went out to do a big deal, intending it to be his last. He ended up in jail with a three-year sentence.

Unknown to Henry, thirty days before he got busted, Rosie prayed, "If You save Henry, I'll give my life back to You."

One night he saw a book that someone had left behind on a bed in the cell. The only light in the cell was shining right down on it. It was a Bible. Since he had nothing else to do, Henry started reading it, and he simply could not get enough. There was a note in the Bible, and written on it was the Sinner's Prayer. Henry thought, "Why not?" and so he prayed for forgiveness. That simple prayer radically changed his life.

Soon Henry had a Bible study in the jail that attracted up to a fourth of the prisoners. He was baptizing people in the showers of the jail.

He would pay a price for his stand for the truth. The inmates set fire to his bed. Thankfully he woke up before he was burned. Henry decided, "God will take care of me. I'm not going to stop."

Henry had been working at a pretty cushy job (by jail standards, at least) in the administration office. A job opened up as janitor at the church on the prison property. Henry took it so he could be in church all day praying for people. He was amazed at how many of the hard-core felons would come and ask him to pray with them in the back of the church.

After his release, Henry and Rosie recommitted their lives to Jesus and stepped into their calling. Along with being successful entrepreneurs, they have been evangelizing as a team for twenty-one years.

Change happens!

This is the purpose of this teaching. The very wind that can push you down can push you through; it can become the force that moves you in the direction God intends for you to go. Let the winds of grace change your sins into wins—for you and for everyone that is linked to your life.

Our beliefs and behaviors do not just impact our lives. The impact continues for generations. If you are looking and searching, you will find the way to change the course of your destiny just as Rahab and Henry and Rosa did.

One of the most important connects you will make with God is the trust you have in His *determined* purpose for your life. You may feel that your life so far has not made sense. You may have experienced pain. Mistakes and failures may have hurt you and those you love. You may feel that God has not given you a fair choice to determine your own destiny.

You can connect with God today and begin to make better choices for your tomorrows. Everything that you do, all the effort required to do right, counts, even when no one is watching. God has set your blood as the secret agent that will carry out the intent and content of your life's movement to the next generation.

CHAPTER 6

Generation Against Generation

The boomers go BOOM! Time to make room.

*When all that generation had been gathered to their
fathers, another generation arose after them who did not
know the Lord nor the work which He had done for Israel.*
—JUDGES 2:10

IT WAS IN MY JUBILEE YEAR—THE YEAR I TURNED FIFTY—WHEN
I began the adventure of writing this, my first published book. It was
a year of researching, writing, and generally driving everyone around
me "legacy crazy"! During the final days as I was in prayer asking
for guidance over the final and most crucial decisions that would be
made regarding the book, something very significant happened. Typi-
cally, I am told, at the end of the "adventure," writers become brain
drained and are finished—literally—with the book. Energy spent,
emotions exhausted, focus faded—the only passion left is to hand it off
to someone else and go run and hide. Don't anyone even whisper the
word *legacy* for at least a month!

During my prayer, I began weeping and felt the fan of the Spirit
sweep over the embers buried under the seemingly cooling ashes of
countless words and rewrites. The fire erupted and danced in wild
passion with even more intensity than I had at the beginning. I felt that
I was not just writing a book but was proclaiming a sound, a trumpet
sounding an alarm to our generation.

This project is not just a manuscript; it's part of a movement—a movement, God forgive my presumption, that *must* happen to save a generation.

The following words may seem harsh. It is a pattern of the way I hear from God. I am probably more thickheaded than most people, and as a result, I often need to be knocked over the head to get the point. If you are expecting a stream of words like water from a drinking fountain, proceed with caution; this might feel more like a fire hydrant.

It was as if I heard the Lord say, "There is a war that is raging—but not like you think. It's a war of *generation against generation*, a battle for the future of the world as you know it." It became clear to me that our country, and cosmos for that matter, is in a battle, a battle not of nation against nation but of generation against generation.

We are in a demographic battle over a generation's soul, not a geographic battle over soil. The weapons of mass deception are death by choice (abortion), divorce (no-fault), debt, and the dumbing down of our moral intelligence.

Who are the casualties of this war?

Our own children—our future generation. Trust has been broken. Covenants mocked. Obligations ignored.

Abortion, abuse, abandonment, and addictions are killing lives, stealing innocence, and destroying the dreams of a generation. These pirates of a generation have raided the safe haven of a mother's womb, the shelter of godly homes, the security of moral absolutes, and so on.

How could we be so blind?

We have allowed new social rules to be written that make it politically incorrect to be correct. We have put up *borders* in our homes and hearts that make it socially illegal to cross into the sacred space of instruction and influence. Everyone has his or her own separate bedroom, bathroom, iPod, computer, cell phone, and friends. Even our church activities have segregated us. We are strangers in our own churches, communities, and the confines of our own homes.

Who is leading this parade? Who are the *they* and *them* who are responsible for this madness? I'm afraid that our own alter egos have stepped outside the boundaries of personal accountability and have taken on lives of their own. We have met the enemy, and it is us! As someone said jokingly, "I am schizophrenic, and so am I." We, on one hand, complain and whine about a life that has been sucked dry of innocence and interest and, on the other hand, succumb to bills, busyness, and malign beliefs that compromise our convictions.

A famous commercial for a national lending firm describes our plight all too well. A man is shown boasting of his nice home, country club membership, luxury cars, and garage filled with every imaginable gadget *not* needed under the sun. Then with a beaming smile he whispers in quiet desperation under his breath, "Help me! Somebody help me! I'm in debt over my head!"

This obsession with self has polarized and paralyzed those who are supposed to be following our example. The generations on both sides of the timeline are bewildered at our behavior. Just where do we think we are going? Why should anyone follow?

Our supposed path of success is paved with the blood of bruised, battered, and broken lives. Powermonger politicians, perverted priests and preachers, and corporate pimps and prostitutes have seduced our character for cash and our virtues for vanity. This kind of behavior has led them astray, leaving only the innocent to pay.

We allowed our children to be fed, bathed, clothed, taught, and nurtured by strangers who have been assigned the task of caregiving. We are treating our parents the same, and unless something changes, we, as baby boomers, will pine away our last days being fed, bathed, clothed, and nurtured by strangers. How strangely ironic!

This is not a book; it's a blast—a trumpet blasting a sound that must awaken us to a life beyond ourselves.

The Purpose-Driven Life, written by my friend Rick Warren, has impacted the lives of over thirty million people. The book planted a seed that our lives only count in the eternal. It successfully argued the case that life here and now is but the dressing room for the stage of eternity. How true—eternally true!

But unfortunately, our spiritual ADD cannot focus very long on the eternal. Eternal matters hold our attention span for only a short time. Like a vague vapor, contrary to the often-quoted scripture in James 4:14, *it's the eternal life* that appears in our mind but for a moment, and then, in the intense heat of the *here and now*, it vanishes away.

I'm calling for a new paradigm that should be added to the mix. I call it the generational-driven life of legacy. This way of living becomes more than a "sweet by-and-by" attempt to bring us to accountability.

With all due respect, eternity should be all we need to be motivated. It should be, but it isn't!

The understanding of a generational life takes on flesh and blood—literally! Children (our own and our communities') become walking and talking reminders that everything about us does matter. When we look at our own life and the lives of others through the lens of legacy we can stay focused on what really matters between here and eternity.

> **If we can link the generational life to our personal life, we may find the motivation that will put us in touch with our eternal life.**

Legacy is a movement that I predict will become a popular buzzword that prayerfully will do more than create a buzz. It will create a blast that will move us from self-centered activities to seed-centered productivity. It has the legs to march us out of the maze and mess we are in and lead us to a better and brighter tomorrow.

Legacy is not an option—it's a divine obligation! Legacy will entice our ego by telling us that we can do more than make a name; we can leave a name. Then legacy will make the ultimate switch and turn our ego from master to servant. It will awaken our eternal conscience and convict our superficial passions.

It's time to grow up!

Legacy is really "purpose" all grown up! It's our mission for becoming mature. The sign of maturity is when we produce more than we consume. What will you leave as your legacy?

Legacy looks for those who still have innocent, idealistic inspiration inside of them. It seeks out people who believe that in the midst of a cynical world there remains unwavering hope that everything we do counts.

Legacy will bring meaning to your means. It will bring some rhyme and reason to the repetitive routine of our present reality. Are you in?

Does anyone sense the rumbling of a movement?

FAMILY TIES OR LIES?

Let me make this clear. Your faith for a legacy will be tested by the next generation. It will be pushed to the limit, kicked against, and walked on and away from. But if you live it, you can leave it. What you believe, you will leave. We need to live what we say we believe because our deeds will be felt in the lives of our seed.

Are you willing to step into a place of action that establishes positive possibilities for your legacy? How far will you let your faith take you into what God has planned for you and your heritage?

In my travels, I often ask people if they would be willing to sacrifice the pleasure of luxuries now for the assurance that their children and grandchildren would be financially secure in the future.

Almost everyone responds with an emphatic yes!

The choice does not have to be either-or, but the willingness to know which one you would choose makes all the difference.

People who love their families respond to the responsibility of a secure financial legacy. What about a proper spiritual legacy? A transfer of material wealth alone could do more harm than good.

Using this book to develop a strong and lasting spiritual legacy will perpetuate the ongoing plan God has for your lineage. Our actions and attitudes carry so much influence. By design or default we are determining a legacy that will have impact on many lives for many generations.

A statement by British poet Michael Roberts—"How can I teach, how can I save this child whose features are my own, whose feet run down the ways that I have walked"—has too often been an indictment rather than an inspiration to me.[1] But I have continued to find the grace to move forward with renewed passion and lead my seed toward a more meaningful legacy.

DREAMS OR SCHEMES?

I want to address a sensitive and perhaps controversial issue. In a society that celebrates individualism over community, we may be fueling a false fire that may end up burning the next generation. It has to do with our telling and selling of dreams.

We talk of dreams as if they can be selected out of a catalog. Images splash across the minds of this generation with no disclaimers of the price or principles that come with dreams. Dreams are in fact the property of God. He is the giver of dreams. They carry not only divine power but also divine purpose. Dreams were meant to connect you to the eternal. Dreams are heaven's hints of God's desires for your life, a life created for His purpose.

They are not a license to do as *you* wish but as *God* wills.

By not holding these principles as a conviction, could we be sending our children down the wrong paths to their purposes?

Here are some examples: "You can be anything you want to be." "If you have the *want to*, you can be anything you want to be." These may be some of the most misleading statements we could give our children.

Though it sounds like an inspiring idea, it can generate more limitations than liberty. How? Let's say you have a nice car and you are told that you can go anywhere you want. The only problem is there are no roads. There you are with this fabulous car and no way of going anywhere, because though the car has power and speed, it needs a road—a path that facilitates its potential. The reverse could be the same—there may be a road, but you do not have the vehicle to make the journey. What good is that road to you?

Simplistic analogy perhaps, but ignoring the principle may lead to complexities that bring more harm than help. Does it make sense to tell our children they can go anywhere and do anything if they have not been given the means to do so? Besides the pain of consistent failures, their disappointments may be linked to their *dis*-appointment with a *determined* purpose that God has equipped them for.

We have to know which dreams we are to hold and which dreams we have been sold. Is it possible to be imprisoned by too many possibilities?

The reason many youth are wandering haplessly through life may be in part because they have been told that they can be *anything* they want. Let's qualify that statement.

You can be the best at what you have been equipped to do. You can go fast and far down *your path* of destiny. You can create unlimited possibilities with the *stuff* you are made of, come from, and born in, but you cannot be whatever you want. Even if you think you have some clever destiny that has no attachment to your lineage, I'm certain that someone in your bloodline set a deed in motion that became a dream seed for you.

How can I say that with such conviction? Because the scripture that I am basing this argument on is crystal clear. God set the time, tribe, and territory for your life. Don't insult your destiny. Your destiny has been in the making for a long time.

I have no intention of taking the romance out of your quest for greatness. Some of you will be called on to take your lineage down a path that will seem outside the expected. You are what I call the "breaker generation." Like Perez, whom we discussed in the beginning of the book, you will break out of the pack and bring your genealogy to a new place—another level.

I am not trying to rain on the parade of possibilities that march through the hearts of the young and innocent. *Au contraire.* God did not make us in haste. God did not make us without a determined and designed purpose. Encouraging the next generation to be "anything they want" needs to be reexamined. Let's give our young people some clear direction and guidance. Telling someone they can do *anything* can be more confining and confusing. Reframe your words, and help them fuel the fires of their true desires. Once they overcome the initial resistance of their natural instincts to do what they want (as we did), they will come to peace with the fact that their lives mean enough to God to be part of a plan that transcends their limited view of time and space.

THIEVES OF DREAMS

When talking about children and the vital role of legacy, many parents are brokenhearted because of strained relationships with their children. I want to talk to you about those struggles. This is not a personal battle you are facing—it's a spiritual war that is affecting us all at some level. As a culture, we are a community family, and we all deal with our society's children. We all have a say in the way the children of our generation turn out. We are not islands. We are all part of the human family. It hurts to see those for whom we have made sacrifices lose their way. It feels like a personal attack when our efforts are ignored or resisted.

Jeannie and I have three grown children, and we have learned many things, often through mistakes. I want to help you avoid mistakes and see the dreams of the next generation come true.

Legacy is the greatest threat to the enemy. Legacy is the backbone not only of a household but also of a nation. Our future as a culture is in the hands of the legacy we give our children. I understand that the battle we rage is complex and filled with variables that cannot be solved with simplistic platitudes and a four-point outline.

But after twelve years in youth ministry and twenty-five years of pastoring, I have detected patterns that consistently undermine legacy. Much could be said about each of the following four deceitful behavioral patterns, but if you can at least identify what they are, you may be able to guard the gates of your legacy with better discernment. Don't be ignorant of Satan's devices.

Rebellion (1 Sam. 15:23)

Rebellion, interestingly enough, is called "witchcraft" in the Bible. This is very appropriate. This attitude paves the way for much heartache for both the child and the parent. During a time when youth are developing some independence, they can be deceived by the act of rebellion masquerading as independence. Ask God for discernment so that you can see the difference and not provoke your children to wrath or rebellion.

Sexual immorality (1 Cor. 5:1–13)

Love for the opposite sex is a natural discovery. Talk more openly about it. Take some of the mystery out of sex by making it something the family can talk about. Don't let Hollywood define sex for our youth. Let sex education be defined in our homes. In fact, a deterrent to defuse the love impersonator of lust is parents talking about how wonderful it is to enjoy the celebrated act of love that comes as a privilege of marriage. It takes the edge off your adolescents' overly charged sexual desires when they are reminded that their parents "do it"! God created sex. Without the spiritual aspect of sexuality, we pervert the purpose of the procreational and recreational gift that sex is to the covenant of marriage.

Sorcery (Rev. 22:15)

Sorcery is the biblical word sometimes used for drugs. (See Revelation 9:21; 18:23.) This trap has been set for our generation with diabolical influence. Satan gains an upper hand when through drugs he has the ability to alter the will of a person. When the will to resist is weakened or compromised with distorted thinking, bondage and brokenness become inevitable. Treat any drug issue you may be facing like it is cancer. Do whatever it takes at any cost to combat and fight this plague quickly. This is a disease that will steal, kill, and destroy your legacy.

Sloth (Prov. 19:15)

Laziness is the by-product of the loss of purpose. When there is no vision, our youth perish (Prov. 29:18). When dreams are denied and vision is vexed, the intoxication of idleness will erode the possibilities of a generation. We are in the midst of a staggering slothfulness that is draining a generation of its potential. I believe that legacy can be a fire that will burn

> **Your legacy may be delayed, but it will not be denied.**

through the cold, cynical hearts of this generation. They are ready to be challenged to hear the call and to step up to a life that will pave a way for their own legacy.

These four forces are being aimed at the next generation. Covertly and overtly we face these evils. Sometimes we can even be an ignorant facilitator. Pray not only that the Lord will protect your household but also that we all as a nation would discern and disarm the weapons that have been launched upon this generation.

If you have felt the pain of these problems in your household, I want you to know that there is hope. God's power is greater than any power that is in the world.

A PARTY FOR THE PRODIGALS

You may be glancing across the table in your dining room, or perhaps on your desk at the office, looking at the pictures of your children and thinking how you long to see your household united in the dreams you once had for them. Oh, how you had such high hopes. But that was then; this is now. But you mustn't lose hope!

Many parents carry heavy hearts for their offspring and wonder if the legacy they planned to leave through their children is in jeopardy. I want to give you hope today, no matter what age your children may be, that the legacy of your seed will prevail. Even if you do not have any biological children, you can be a part of this desperately needed *coming-home* party of our wayward ones.

Because of issues like abortion, abuse, abandonment, and addictions, many of this generation have become what the Bible calls "prodigals." I'm going to assume that you know the story. If not, may I suggest that you take the time to read it in Luke 15.

In the passage, Jesus speaks of parables about lost possessions and people. There are *things* (wealth, property, earthly possessions) we lose that can be recovered. There are *people* (marriages, relationships) we lose who can be restored, such as children's connection to the faith.

These stories of hope provide lessons on how we can become an instrument in the miracle of the lost being found.

The prodigal son insisted on taking his inheritance while in his youth. He left home and engaged in riotous living. He wasted his equity, or inheritance, and very quickly began to mount up a debt of iniquity, or sin.

Once he lost his money, the loss of his friends and dignity quickly followed. He ended up eating at a trough with pigs. For a Jew, this was the ultimate disgrace. At this point, he saw the gap between what he had left (his heritage) and what he had left (his losses)—and the gap was painfully wide. When the awful consequences of his choices were realized, he went from a give-me-what-I-want to a make-me-a-servant mind-set.

He now wanted to come home. He was ready for a change. He realized that the life he had rejected wasn't as bad as he had thought. Daddy's intelligence had improved, or maybe it was his perception of his dad, but things definitely looked different from the pigpen.

When he eventually returned, it was not a total surprise to the father. Get this—the father was prepared for the miracle. He had shown patience. He was ready to celebrate what he had never given up on—his son's homecoming.

There was a sequence of events that led to the prodigal son's humbling return home—protection, patience, and preparation for a party. Deconstructing this sequence will help us deal with our own prodigals.

PROTECT THE GATES

The father did not go after his son while he was in the pigpen. Get that. That wisdom may be the most crucial nugget of the story. Do not attempt to save a child who is not ready to be saved.

We must protect the home for the time when our child returns. Too many parents go after their children while risking their own sanity, livelihood, marriage, and/or other children in the home. (We are speaking of children who are at the age of accountability.)

Protect your home with your morals. God holds you responsible to establish and uphold standards in your home. There is nothing wrong with taking a stand. Parents today need strong moral muscles. When you let your guard down, you let your children down. Morals eventually create morale.

Never compromise the standards of your home. You have the right and responsibility to guard and protect the atmosphere so it is congruent with the morals you believe in. Your children may resist and even attack what you have established, but don't let them tear down the very gates they will want to establish in their own homes someday.

Our culture is also an instrument of legacy. It is very difficult to uphold the morals that have kept our legacy intact for so many generations in the loose culture we see today. At some point, we need to expand beyond our personal well-being to evaluate the condition of our country. All of us—single, married, with or without children—are building a national legacy. Are we funding and fueling a culture that we will be ashamed of a few decades from now? For example, could you be funding MTV (the controversial media empire) or other controversial society shapers with your portfolio? You might be surprised who is funding the corruption everyone is screaming about.

We are all gatekeepers for the next generation.

Patience With Joy

Guard your thoughts. Find a way to keep the joy of life and of the Lord in your heart. Your heart is yours, and no one else is capable of taking ownership of it. Let your children see that you are happy. Don't let them see you sweat. The smell of the pigpen will get to them more quickly if you don't have a stinky attitude.

Don't take it personally. Let me say that again—don't take it personally. When our children are going through their stuff, it is very selfish of us to make it about our feelings and our reputation. When your children see that you care about them, and that it is not about you or your reputation, you will gain much more influence and walk through the process more quickly. It's a good thing not to take all the credit for how good your children have turned out—but don't take all the blame either.

There is a long lineage that has had its influence on who and what your children are becoming. Do your part, and trust the power of the blood to do its part.

Don't fret about what others are thinking about your children. Your peers will not be there for you in the midnight hours when you are dealing with the consequences of your children's choices, nor will they want to interrupt their busy schedules to come to the party when your prodigal son or daughter comes home.

Check your panic gauge. Learn to keep a balanced perspective where you evaluate what is going on based on a scale of one to ten (ten being murder). Sure, it's irritating that he slammed the door after you grounded him. Sure, it was rude that she didn't call when she was going to be an hour past curfew. But it is not an eight, nine, or ten.

They will try to break your heart into a million pieces. Then when they come home, and they *will* come home to God, you won't have the heart to celebrate. No one will be more sad than the very child you let break your heart.

Develop a thick skin so you can keep a tender heart.

Preparation for a Party

I believe that the prayers of a parent are powerful. God will find a way to answer your prayers. If there is a prayer at stake, He can and He will *make them* do what is right.

Prayer is a powerful force in the heart of a parent. When a prayer is spoken on behalf of our seed, the calculated commentaries of our theology seem to crumble. God has no problem messing up our well-versed opinions on the sovereignty of His will and man's free will. God seems more interested in answering our prayer than He is in answering to our theology.

> The anointed prayer of a parent avails much.
> —James 5:16, author's paraphrase

I realized how sophisticated the military has become when I read about "smart bombs." These bombs, unlike "dumb bombs," can hit a specific target with astonishing accuracy. Military troops on the ground will secretly mark or paint a target. The bombs are then dropped using radar to guide them to the marked target. The smart bomb will move and maneuver over any and all obstacles, circling and for great lengths of time searching out the target until it hits the mark.

As I was reading this article, I exploded with a revelation (pun intended). The word *anointing* in the Bible speaks of oil being *smeared*, *marked*, and even *painted* on an object. As we pray with an anointing for our children, we are "marking" and "painting" them for God to do His will in their lives. Pray with a vision of your child (or anyone else for that matter) being "marked" as you pray. "Lord, they are Yours. You brought them through me. You have a plan for their lives, and even though they don't see it, I know that it will 'hit" them soon, and they will return to the designed destiny for their lives."

Put the mark on your children. They belong to God and to the perpetual legacy that is in their destiny. Everyone can use this "marking" power while praying. Even if you don't have "covenant" children, you can engage in prayers for the children in your extended family, your community, or your church. The times demand a call to prayer. Parents many times lose patience and lose faith and become fearful over the fate of their children. Too often my own prayers for my children were nothing more than worry covered in religious words. I was just worrying out loud. Sometimes I can pray more effectively for other people's children than for my own. Are you willing to pray for someone else's legacy?

The day finally came when the father's prayers were answered. The prodigal son said, "I will arise and go to my father, and will say to him…'*Make* me like one of your hired servants'" (Luke 15:18–19, emphasis added). God can indeed "make" our children come home.

Don't panic if your children seem to be determining just how low they can go. Don't worry if they are eating out of the pig trough. God is with them right now wherever they are, nudging and even nagging until your prayers can be marked "answered." His predetermined purpose will be made known. When you look at it from a biblical view, those children are His, not yours, and God cares for them even more than you do. That's a good thing.

The most encouraging part of the parable of the prodigal son is that the father was not just prepared and patient, but he anticipated the party that was to come.

"Don't touch that calf! That's going to be our meal for the party we will be having when my son comes home. That robe I've been ironing every day is also for my boy. I have the band ready. I've been taking dance lessons because it is going to be one great party when my son comes home."

He never gave up. He ran to greet his son when he saw him walking toward home. He had envisioned this day, prepared for this day, waited patiently for this day.

Can you see your children coming back to God? Can you smell the barbecue? Can you hear the band tuning up? The victory happens first in your prayer of faith. See it and seize it now.

Most of us have been through our own prodigal story. It may have been your own children, a relative, a close friend, or even yourself who was the fallen one in your own prodigal story.

For Father's Day a few years ago, my son gave me a card that was funny—kind of. It read:

Dad, I'm afraid I didn't show my appreciation of how great you are when I was young. I'm going to make it up to you! Get my room ready. I'm quitting my job and moving back home to devote all my energy to you!

You too will see God's blessing on your life. The children that you are concerned about right now will come home. Be patient. The party will happen. Guard the gates, and know that the party will happen.

This statement from a preacher reminds me of my own life:

When I was growing up, I had a drug problem. I was "drug" to church every time the doors were open. I was "drug" to read the Bible and pray. I was "drug" to youth camp, and I was "drug" to outreach ministries. It did not matter if I wanted to go or not. I was "drug." That addiction has remained stronger than heroin, cocaine, alcohol, immorality, and other vices. I can't get it out of my system. I can't get it out of my mind.

Amen! Because I was "drug" to church, I am a "victim" of a near-thirty-year happy marriage, three fantastic adult children and an incredible son-in-law, a ministry of over thirty years, and more blessing than you have the time to hear.

Train up a child in the way he should go,
And when he is old he will not depart from it.
—PROVERBS 22:6

PAVING PARADISE:
THE LOSS OF THE FAMILY TREE

Many have lost the shade of their family tree. Have you?

Maybe you have faced a divorce, or a divide (geographically or emotionally), or even a death in your family. These painful events can cause you to stop caring or to grow weary of carrying on a legacy. Are you tired of the battle? Just pave over your family tree and put up a parking lot. It's less hassle.

> ...lest any root of bitterness springing up cause trouble, and by this many become defiled.
>
> —Hebrews 12:15

What can we do to keep our family trees from becoming defiled and destroyed?

How can we keep from wanting to cut down the tree whose shade we have lived under? As a culture, when we allow the destruction of our individual family trees, we will eventually feel the effect on our community family forest. We endanger our very survival. I know that some face such complex and condemning circumstances. But if there were ever a reason to insist and persist, it's for our family legacy now and for the generations to come. Don't be so quick to pave that paradise and put up a parking lot.

No matter how hard it may be, do what must be done to nurture the trees that have taken generations to grow. Water them in love; prop them up with constant encouragement. Keep the bulldozers of despair and disappointment from tearing them down.

You do this by reminding yourself that everywhere you go you take the past legacy of your parents and the potential legacy of your children with you. Think of this when you are tempted to engage in a questionable activity. Would you cheat on your taxes and bring shame on your parents? Would you view pornography with your children in the room? A multigenerational mind-set provides the strength to walk away—not just because you do not want to harm yourself, but because you know it would be a terrible thing to do to them.

Your legacy "seed" are with you always. Through the blood, we are always connected, influencing future generations. I am certain that if we really understood this we would find the stamina to resist and refuse to stoop to negative and destructive behavior.

Every temptation we face can become a stronghold of destructive behavior in our bloodline unless we trust Christ to help us. Satan finds a toehold in our imagination and attitudes and wiggles that toe until it becomes a foothold in our actions. Soon he has a stronghold of attributes and characteristics that find their way into our seed.

The more I learn about DNA, the more I see the brilliance of the power and purpose of the blood. In 1993, under the direction of the

United States Army Intelligence and Security Command (INSCOM), white blood cells scraped from the mouth of a volunteer were centrifuged and placed in a test tube. A probe from a polygraph—a lie (or emotion) detector—was then inserted in the tube. The donor of the cheek cells was seated in a room separated from his donated cells and shown a television program with many violent scenes. When the volunteer watched scenes of fighting and killing, the probe from the polygraph detected extreme excitement in the mouth cells—even though they were in a room down the hall! It appears that DNA carries our emotions and reactions, even when separated from our body.

Repeated experiments produced the same response, even up to fifty miles in distance and two days after the cells were removed.[2] Bizarre? It may be more biblical than we realize!

Your DNA cries out into future generations. What will your blood be saying? What will you be adding to the lineage that is yet to come?

The fact that *in every deed there is a seed* is not meant to intimidate you but to show you how you can create a legacy through your children for future generations. One woman told me, "My children are grown, and so I no longer need to be concerned about the whole 'deed-to-seed' thing." However, I believe that until the very day you pass from this life, you have a direct line of influence to your children through the generational link of the blood. As you study this book and pray, you are making an investment into the legacy account of your family and into the family of God.

> **Our death is not an end if we can live on in our children and the younger generation. For they are us; our bodies are only wilted leaves of the tree of life.**
>
> **—Albert Einstein**

When you pass to the other side, you become eternally linked through the "great cloud of witnesses" that will continue to leave your personal "witness" of legacy for generations. (See Hebrews 12:1–2.)

Live your life with a deeper meaning than just for the moment. Live for a cause that taps into the needs and opportunity that make a difference for our world. Be determined to leave more than you take. Your kids will get it. Don't worry that they don't seem to be listening to what you are saying; they are distracted by what you are doing. Do right and trust the blood to do its work. More is caught than taught. It will catch on.

Human nature does not live by deciding to do right based on moral maxims, rules and regulations, or even fear of consequences. We rarely decide—we discern how we will live our lives (especially youth). Our perception becomes our reception, which determines our lifestyle. What we learn through our experiences and examples will trump education every time. Your behavior carries in your biology the power to affect the beliefs of the next generation. Trust the blood.

"I Was Here!"

As an ambitious (actually, rebellious) young man, my brother Joe did something that almost landed him in jail. We were visiting spectacular Mount Rushmore in the Black Hills of South Dakota. Joe had the cool idea to carve his name on one of the trees in this national forest.

When approached by a federal officer, it was hard to deny the crime; he had carved "I was here" along with his name and the place where he was from. Thankfully, a sincere apology from him and my parents brought a peaceful resolve.

We all have this urge to carve out our name on the family tree of humanity. How can we live in a way that assures us we are part of the ongoing story of the human family? How do we make our mark of "I was here"?

The Bible declares our lives to be "trees of righteousness." We are growing and living our lives as part of our family tree. What begins as a seed grows into a tree whose fruit and shade are enjoyed for generations.

"I was here" is another way of saying, "Thy kingdom has come—in me—as it is in heaven." We all want to make our mark on life. That's not only natural; it's a necessity.

Let your "I am a-gene-nation" run wild through heaven's field of dreams. See your life rooted like a fruitful tree that others will partake of for generations. Your significance may seem small, like the significance of one single tree in a forest. That tree may never be seen or celebrated as distinct from the rest of the trees it lives among. But it only seems that way. In reality every tree has a distinct purpose.

I read recently about trees in the Great Basin in the western United States. They are some of the oldest living trees on earth. One of these trees has been named "Methuselah" because it is 4,723 years old.

Think about what that tree has lived through. It was standing during the building of the pyramids, the ministry of Christ, and the rise and fall of many nations.

That's what a legacy does. It stands long after the winds of change have calmed. It stands through the fires and the floods. It stands!

Are you committed to being part of a legacy that will be like a tree of righteousness? There may need to be some pruning. Have the courage to make decisions that will bring longevity to your tree.

However, resist the urge to plow and pave over your past. Too many people have cut themselves off from a deep-rooted heritage. They squandered their legacy and interrupted a pattern for those in the future.

A research was conducted in 1877 into the life of Max Juke, a vocal atheist who lived a godless life and married an ungodly woman. Of his 540 direct descendants and more than 700 distant relatives, 310 were professional paupers, 7 murderers, 60 habitual thieves, and 130 frequently convicted criminals. Only 20 of the 1,200 learned a trade, and 10 of those learned it in a state prison.[3]

In 1898, Dr. Whiship wanted to study a desirable family to offset the findings about Max Juke, so he selected Jonathan Edwards, a godly man who married a godly woman. He was the founder of a family of more than 1,400 noblemen. More than 120 graduates of Yale were direct descendents, 13 became college presidents, more than 100 were college professors, and several descendents have been among the most illustrious men of their time.[4] At least 100 became ministers, 75 became army officers, 30 were judges, 100 were lawyers, 80 became public officials, 3 became congressmen, 2 were U.S. senators, and 1 became vice president of the United States.[5]

Your determined desire to make a difference *will* make a difference! Just remember that it takes generations to build a legacy!

CHAPTER 7

Spot Removal for Genes
Prewashed genes available

Though your sins are like scarlet, they shall be as white as snow.
—ISAIAH 1:18

A CONVICTION OF RAPE IN 1982 WOULD HAVE COST A FIFTY-YEAR-OLD Dallas man nearly half his life in prison. However, he petitioned for retesting of the state's rape evidence in 1989 and redoubled his efforts in 2001 after Texas passed a law granting postconviction access to DNA testing. He said, "The Lord kept pushing me because I wanted my name back!" After spending more than ten years behind bars, he was paroled in 1993. He was completely exonerated by DNA testing. In the aftermath of the new evidence, prosecutors joined defense lawyers in calling for his clearing.

The man got his good name back because of the availability of DNA testing. Through use of a previously unavailable technology, it was found that genetic material recovered from the victim conclusively excluded him.[1]

It thrills me to hear those stories. The blood became the greatest witness to the man's innocence. As of April 2007, two hundred prisoners have been exonerated because of DNA testing.[2]

A greater story is how the blood of Christ set us free from our past in spite of our guilt! Christ has left His blood on the scene of our crimes of deception and disobedience. It's as if *He* committed the crime. "He made Him who knew no sin to be sin for us, that we might become the righteousness of God" (2 Cor. 5:21).

Once you've made your appeal to the courts of heaven, you are exonerated from your past and can be free of your sins and the guilt that torments you. You can live guilt free and have a God-given confidence.

The blood Christ gave for us carries more scriptural and scientific knowledge than we were aware of just a generation ago. Because of this breakthrough, the Scriptures can now be understood in a whole new light. We can look at words like *the blood, inheritance, seed, generations,* and—a very key subject—*iniquity* with greater insight.

Iniquity infects your DNA for bad. Equity infuses your DNA for good. The past iniquity of your life and lineage can be scrubbed clean. Grace becomes the spot removal for genes.

Iniquity becomes an important link to understanding our legacy.

What is iniquity, and what impact does it have on our lives?

Iniquity is defined in Bible commentaries as wickedness and sinfulness and that which is associated with the sins of our fathers. Basically, it is the wicked, weak, and wayward characteristics that are transferred from one generation to the next. Iniquity is sin's visitation rights to your lineage. That right extends up to four generations (Exod. 20:5).

According to the Bible, and even our own conscience, we have all sinned and fallen short of the glory—the target—of God's best for our lives. We carry this guilt as a result of the weight and taint of sin we have inherited. We came into this world wearing "Adam's genes." These genes are "formed and shaped" in iniquity. We were born sinners.

And sinners do what sinners do—sin! That's only half the problem. Sin is not just what we *do* wrong—it's what we *are* that's wrong. The sin condition is not just about what we do—it's what we are. It's not just an event; it's a condition.

We need a cure for our rage, bitterness, brokenness, prejudice, selfishness, pride, lust, greed, perversion, hurt, hopelessness, evil imagination, and confusion.

Are we now victims of our past, carrying the "dirty" genes of our deeds and the seeds of those who came before us? Are we trapped in this tainted bloodline forever? Does our DNA doom us?

There is hope.

The gospel is the good news that the blood of Christ is available to transform and conform our past. The accumulating debt of our iniquity will not cause us to become spiritually bankrupt or impair our ability to achieve our destiny. Our debt has been paid. (See Isaiah 53:3–10.)

God has provided a way to interrupt the natural sequence of events that would otherwise have made us victims. We can escape from the deserved consequences of the unwise decisions and/or the behavior of our past. Christ can cleanse you from every thought or act of unrighteousness and give you a fresh start—a clean slate—that will change your entire perspective on life. A new pair of *prewashed genes* is available for you.

Are you ready to make that change?

By the blood of Adam's one act of sin, man became flawed and fragile. By the blood of Christ's one act of sacrifice, man became sanctified and strong.

It's spot removal for genes.

What do you think of when you hear the word *spot*? Is it that greasy stain on your favorite tie? A nasty smudge on the dress or suit you wanted to wear tonight?

The spot I'm referring to is one that stains your genes, a spot that can be replicated for generations.

The Greek text of the Bible actually uses the word *spot* to refer to sin. The spot of sin must be removed before we can stand before God and man with confidence. Sin is the spot that must be dealt with as you move forward to claim your legacy: "How much more shall the blood of Christ, who through the eternal Spirit offered Himself *without spot* to God, cleanse your conscience...?" (Heb. 9:14, emphasis added).

That promise is portrayed in the simple song we sang as children, "Mary Had a Little Lamb."

Jesus was that little lamb, and because He was sinless, His fleece was white as snow. I am fascinated by the study of lambs and their blood as it relates to the redemption plan of God for us.

The imagery of animal sacrifices is morbid and cruel. It's meant to show us the innocence lost and the price to be paid for our acts of sin. The point is made: "All we like sheep have gone astray" (Isa. 53:6).

Innocence lost.

Through the blood of Christ, we can infuse a whole new genetic code to get our innocence back.

Innocence found.

The Lamb of God has saved us from the serpent's venom of sin, much as lives are saved today from the venom of poisonous snakebites by the blood of lambs. First, the venom is extracted from a live snake. The snake releases venom from its fangs, which are draped over the lip of a cup. The venom is collected in the glass cup. Once enough venom has been extracted, it is bottled and sent off to a lab. At the lab, a sheep is injected with 1/10 to 1/100 the lethal dose of venom.

Over a period of several weeks, the sheep is injected with increasingly potent doses of venom. The animal's body produces antibodies, which are proteins made by the body to fight foreign substances (such as venom). When injected into someone that has been bitten, the needed resistance becomes possible.[3]

This is what Christ, the Lamb of God, did for you and me: He became sin (He did not commit sin). Christ took the poison of sin and absorbed it into His blood. Through faith, when we apply the blood, we can resist the *venom* of the serpent and live above the consequences we could expect from our sinful deeds. We have power over sin through the blood of Christ.

The power of legacy is based on the truth that I want to reaffirm to you. Christianity is not just a belief. It's a behavior transformation. Through Christ, we don't just have the guilt of sin taken away. He has taken the nature of sin consciousness away. We are changed. We act differently because we *are* different. Mankind needed more than just a positive mental attitude adjustment.

No clever arrangement of rotten eggs can ever make a good omelet. We needed and received a new *egg*—a new birth. Christ was the original Easter egg! Through Him we are born again by that incorruptible seed.

So why didn't God come down from heaven and wipe out our sins with one merciful sweep? Why through a virgin did He have to reduce Himself to the size of a cell in Mary's womb? Why did He need to become a man?

The answer?

Because of the blood! The same blood that was meant to transfer the goodness from one generation to the next also became the source that carried the virus of Adam and Eve's sin.

It would take the spotless Lamb who was white as snow to save us. God would not only forgive us but also forge in us a new clean slate to build our lives upon.

But why do we struggle with negative and even destructive behavior *after* our conversion? I want to tackle this issue. We need to see that our new spiritual nature will require nurturing. Just as the debate is heated and divided over the issue of nature versus nurture among scientists, so it is with our spiritual nature versus nurture issues among theologians. I am neither a scientist nor a theologian, but I am living out the wonder of this marvelous promise of redemption every day, and I believe I can help you see that it too is a life based on nature *via* nurture, not nature versus nurture.

BREAKING THE CURSE OR THE COURSE?

The Scriptures are clear concerning our past sins. We become free of our past and released from the curse that sin has had on our lives. We don't need to search out generational curses to live a life that is free and pure. Digging up curses can be a tragic waste of your energy. Every curse is broken when Jesus comes into your heart.

We have a new *course* that we can build our lives upon. We get all the good that's in our lineage, yet the bad is removed. What a deal!

The *curse* of a sinful nature was broken off our lives, and a new nature was given to us. "Christ has redeemed us from the curse of the law, having become a curse for us" (Gal. 3:13).

Removing the *curse* was Christ's job. That's a done deal for those of us who have accepted Christ and His "Divine Nature Applied." Correcting your *course* is your job. The *power* of sin has already been broken. Breaking the *pattern* of sinful habits is your responsibility. It is essential that you understand the difference between the two. One is in the spiritual realm; the other is in the soul's realm (your will, thoughts, and emotions).

There is a power that Satan had over you before you were saved. That power has been rebuked, stopped, and broken. Now the challenge is having the will to deal with your thought and emotional behavior patterns.

We carry many wonderful instincts that can be positive and hold potential for our future. It's in most of us to want to be good, to be kind, to love and be loved. In and of itself, this is good. We also have negative instincts like jealousy, anger, and selfishness. If followed, they will delay or distract and ultimately destroy the plans God has for you and your generational influence. All it takes is just a slight negative influence to taint all the good intentions that we have. Sin has had its way with our human nature. And even though the power of sin is broken, the old patterns have been deeply embedded in our soul.

You have become a new person through Christ, but you still live in the same house (your mind and body). You have old habits and thought patterns that have *rented* your space for many years. And yes, some of these patterns are generational.

I'm told that amputees have strange sensations in the very area where the part of their body has been amputated. Even though it's no longer there, they may feel the need to scratch or move their leg or arm. The mind is still using the same wiring system for the body after our conversion. In time that sensation will go away, or at least we will no longer feel the need to respond to it.

This begins to explain the difference between the *curse* of sin's power and the *course* that sin's path has led us down.

This is why you must renew your mind every day. The *old man of sin* has been cut off. But your mind has been trained to send and receive messages from that old nature. In time, you too will no longer need or want to respond.

Meanwhile, you'll need to reprogram your mind and body to your new spiritual life. It's like pressing the delete button on your computer. You will have areas where deep negative patterns have been programmed in you or in your lineage. Don't confuse the distinction between what Christ has already done and what you will need to do. The line can be blurry sometimes, but if you fail to accept by faith what has already been done, you run the risk of insulting the work of grace in your heart. (See Romans 6.)

A preacher made a deal with a young man who was trading a lawn mower for a bike. After the deal was made, the preacher could not get the lawn mower motor to start.

"You'll have to cuss at it to get it started," the young man said.

"Oh, I don't cuss. I haven't used a foul word in years," replied the preacher.

The young man responded, "Trust me—it will come back to you!"

Sometimes, the old way of living comes back to you.

Remember, you may sin, but you are not a sinner. You may lie, but you are not a liar. You may have moments of defeat, but you are not defeated.

As we have said, you are born again by the incorruptible Word of God. Your new DNA nature will need to be nurtured. Your belief in this truth activates the wonder-working power of the blood. But there is still some work to do.

Each of us has instincts and tendencies created or supported by our inherited DNA to slant or tilt toward certain behavior patterns. The characteristics inherited from the accumulated

> **Your choice becomes a voice to the next generation.**

actions of our forefathers cannot be ignored or denied. Know what the tendencies and the tilt of your genetics are. You can't just let your old nature have its course. It will get you in trouble if you don't develop a resistance to it.

The scary campfire legend is told of the babysitter who calls the police because of a persistent caller, only to be told to get out of the house immediately because the tap placed on the phone revealed that the call was coming from inside the house. This reminds us that this can become our own horror story; sometimes the enemy is *in* the house. Our own negativity distracts from the work of the cross. Our soul needs daily and determined renewal. The greatest enemy may very well be *in-a-me*.

Renew your mind. Reestablish your trust in the curse being broken. You may have an issue with pride or vanity. The core of sin is always harbored by the ego. Ego is the god we create in our own image. I always say, "The lust of the flesh and eyes will get you into trouble, but it will be pride that keeps you there."

You may be dealing with destructive behavior patterns of obsessions and addictions. This is mischanneled passion. As you focus your attention on the plans God has for you, you will find the negative obsessions' power over you diminishing. Your darkness will dissipate as you get it out into the light.

Your spirit man was immediately transformed at conversion. Your thoughts, will, and emotions are *being* "transformed by the renewing of your mind" (Rom. 12:2). The mind and body go through a process as you walk out your faith. As you come into complete alignment with your spirit man, you will experience what I call a "whole in one." That's when your spirit, soul, and body are in unity. "Now may the God of peace Himself *sanctify you completely*; and may your *whole spirit, soul, and body* be preserved blameless at the coming of our Lord Jesus Christ" (1 Thess. 5:23, emphasis added).

> **The belief of "I can't" comes from the belief that "I'm not."**

Our position of right standing with God is not in question. It's the process that must be walked out between our *position*—how God sees us—and our *practice*—how we see ourselves (which is how others will see us).

God allows you to be a partaker. We become joint heirs, partners in the construction business of legacy. As you receive and respond to the working of the Word, you close the gap and begin to see the fruit of your obedience manifested in your daily life.

What started as a work of the *charisma* of the Holy Spirit has now become the workings of your *character*. From "grace to guts" you have renewed your mind (will, thoughts, and emotions) with the Word of God. You have made the right choices day in and day out. That transformation is what you can now transfer to your seed.

Will of Choice or Free Will?

The earth is suspended between the tension of the magnetic North Pole and South Pole, much as our lives are suspended between the tension of good and evil. It is our responsibility to choose which end we will gravitate toward.

Although this freedom to choose is called *free will*, it is not really free at all. "Free" insinuates something we can have without cost. Nothing is free. You have free will to choose, but you will pay the consequence of your choice. The consequences will affect you either now or later. Or it will affect somebody else now. Or it will affect somebody else later.

The power to choose carries more influence than any other power on the earth. Even though you cannot avoid life's consequences, you are not helplessly forced to sit on the sidelines and just watch life happen to you. You have power. What you make happen, what you allow to happen, and how you respond to what happens are the authority of the will of choice.

Your choices can have impact for generations. Choose or lose!

In Eugene H. Peterson's book *Reversed Thunder*, he speaks with piercing insight into the need for choosing to live holy. "Holy living is posited in the conviction that everything we do, no matter what we do, however common and little noticed in our lives, is connected with the action of God and is seed that becomes either a harvest of holiness or a vintage of wrath!"[4]

When God placed Adam and Eve in the garden, He gave them choices and made it clear there would be consequences to their choices. "But of the tree of the knowledge of good and evil you shall not eat, *for in the day that you eat of it you shall surely die*" (Gen. 2:17, emphasis added).

When Adam took a bite of the fruit of the forbidden tree, it became a byte of sin. A virus was released into the program of all of our DNA chips. This gene germ is the origin of the disease of sin.

Our bodies live with germs. The tension of germs keeps our defense mechanisms strong. The world system is much like our bodies. We live in a world that is in a constant tension of good and evil. This keeps us on our toes—or, quite literally, on our knees.

The human family has paid for the choice Adam and Eve made in the Garden of Eden. Because of that sin, we who have come from one blood have had to bear the burden of a sinful nature.

Get Yourself Back to the Garden

Most of us begin our lives with great dreams. If we were so blessed, we spent our childhood in the *garden of naïveté* and were immersed in uninhibited expectations of what might be.

Then, like Adam and Eve in Genesis 3, we were seduced out of the garden by lust and lies, by temporary pleasures and pride. Looking back from the outside of the garden is a painful awakening. How can we get ourselves back to the garden?

There is a way. We will learn how by reminding ourselves how we, as Adam and Eve's descendants, got kicked out in the first place.

After Adam and Eve sinned, they hid themselves in the garden. Do we think that we can hide our sins from God?

God cried out to Adam and said, "Adam, where are you?" It wasn't because God did not know the place where they were in the garden. God knew the place; He was looking for the *position* of purpose they had drifted from.

God still cries out today, "Where are you?"

Adam's statement to God, "We were naked and ashamed," continues to be the repeated line for mankind. When we are out of place, we feel naked and ashamed.

"Who told you that you were naked?" God asked.

We are always battling the voices that are telling us what we are supposed to be: "Who told you that you were not good enough?" "Who told you that you were too big, too small, too dark, too poor, too *whatever*?"

Images are constantly being flashed before us. We are always feeling like we are not quite good enough unless we wear these clothes, drive this car, live in this home, and vacation in that resort. Television, magazines, movies, and billboards all distort the right view of who we were destined by God to be.

We cover ourselves, never comfortable with what we truly are. We strive to look and act like the person someone else is telling us to be. Who are *they* whom we are always trying to please?

We seem to never be quite comfortable in our own skin.

Look deep inside, and listen to the voice in the garden of your inner man. Hear the sounds of confidence. Hear the voice of God: "It is He who has made us, and not we ourselves; we are His people and the sheep of His pasture" (Ps. 100:3). It is He who knows you best and loves you most.

Come back to the garden. Come back to where, when, and who you were destined by God to be. Nobody can compete with being you. You are the best you there will ever be. The day you really believe that is the day you get back to the garden. Iniquity no longer dominates your life. In the garden, you can grow equity. You can even turn your iniquity into equity.

Unbreaking Your Heart: It Can Hurt for Good

God can take the biggest mistakes and failures of your past and use them to prepare and lead you to your own distinct ministry. You will be tempted to run from or numb your painful past. But surprisingly, there is some good that can come from your bad past. The passion and the purpose you long for has a connection to your pain. What you are looking for to turn your life around may be closer than you think. Close to home. Close to a part of your life you may not be comfortable with. Your past can hurt for good.

You may need to turn your hurt into an instrument of healing for someone else. It may be the legacy link you have been searching for.

Kathleen is a friend of mine who turned her most miserable moment of pain into a miraculous ministry of gain. Kathleen came from a family with a multigenerational pattern of alcoholism and gambling. She found the tenacity to resist and had good success running construction crews of more than two hundred fifty workers. Married, divorced, and a twenty-seven-year-old single *career* mom with a one-year-old baby, the last thing she needed was to become pregnant.

She became pregnant.

Trying to *save face* as the strong one, she hid this from her family. Kathleen sought and followed the advice of the popular and persuasive family planning organization that was easily accessible. Ironically the *choice not* to have an abortion was not offered as an alternative.

She followed her head and ignored her heart. She had the baby aborted.

Afterward, she walked out the back door and discovered that her car had a flat tire. With no one she could call and no place to go, she sat down on the curb. As the realization of what she had done sank into her disturbed heart, she began to cry. She could not stop her body from rocking back and forth, and her crying turned to wailing for what she had left behind in the abortion clinic.

That was the moment that changed her life.

Within a year, she had walked away from everything that she previously thought was important. How could she have given up her child for her job and material success?

That would never happen again to her—or to anyone else if she could help it.

Kathleen began volunteering at clinics and speaking to postabortive women about the emotional issues they face. Eventually she founded Birth Choice Health Clinics.[5] Kathleen's mission is to "compete for the lives of women and their children." The clinic Kathleen had her baby aborted at turned the ultrasound screen away. If only she could have heard the baby's heart, she might have heard her own. At Birth Choice, the woman sees her baby and hears the heartbeat. She is given the full support she needs to make an informed decision. Part of the postabortive counseling women receive is an opportunity to name their baby and then give the baby to Jesus. Kathleen took the tragedy of her abortion and gave her baby a name—Toby! Birth Choice founded Toby's House to provide shelter and care for pregnant women in crisis. Kathleen's act of testimony has helped thousands of mothers and fathers avoid or be healed of the trauma of an abortion.

Turn your wounds into weapons. Learn to turn what the enemy meant for evil into good for the kingdom of God. Choose to let your hurt be for good.

Little Johnny stood at the sickbed of his sister who was dying from a rare blood disease. He had survived the same illness some months prior and had developed the antibodies required to fight the disease. Unfortunately, the little girl's immune system was unable to form the antibodies, and her condition worsened by the minute.

There was hope, however. The little brother had the same blood type as his sister. His healthy blood, containing the antibodies, could destroy the disease before it took the life of his sister. There wasn't much time. The doctors would quickly need to draw blood from Johnny and transfuse it into the sister if she was going to survive.

Quickly, the doctor explained the situation to him and asked if he would be willing to give his blood to his sister. The little boy swallowed nervously, hesitated momentarily, then looked into the doctor's eyes and said, "If it will save my sister, I'll do it."

"That's a brave boy," said the doctor, patting the boy on the arm. The boy lay next to his sister during the transfusion. As her skin recovered its natural rosy hue, the boy smiled. Then the boy's eyes filled with tears. He blinked rapidly, trying to fight them back. "Are you uncomfortable?" asked the doctor. "Does it hurt?"

The little boy shook his head. "No, sir," he said with a wavering voice, "but when will I start to die?"

The little boy had misunderstood the doctor. He believed that for his sister to recover, he would have to give her all his blood. He was prepared to give his life for his sister.

Our elder brother, Christ, *did* give His blood and life for us. That blood not only saved us but also has given us the miraculous opportunity to take our past sins and the sins of our forefathers and experience a fresh start.

BREAKING THE COURSE OF YOUR PAST

I want to lead you in a prayer that will set you free from the iniquity influence over your life. Pray this from your heart:

> *I cannot undo my past. I cannot allow myself to be victimized by the biological and behavioral patterns of my life. There is a way of escape—a supernatural transformation through Jesus Christ. By faith I accept the characteristics of Christ. His blood carries the power to cleanse and to change. I am being changed into the image of the Son of God by the power of the seed of God that is in me. I will live my life with the realization that in every deed there is a seed. I accept the challenge to live not just for me, not just for now, but for my generational and eternal responsibilities. By the blood of the Lamb and the word of my testimony, I will overcome. In Jesus's name, amen.*

PART THREE

Your Present

Legacy is not just about what you've become. It's about facing God with what you've done. Protecting and projecting your legacy is life's purpose.

CHAPTER 8

Bonding or Bondage?

Fit to be tied

No, I will not break my covenant; I will not take back a single word I said.

—Psalm 89:34, nlt

"I'm out of here!" Jeannie said sternly during a heated discussion.

The pressures of marriage were not fusing us together very well. It was more like lighting a fuse that was about to blow Jeannie and I apart.

We all face times of extraordinary challenge, times that strain the marriage covenant nearly to its breaking point. Years ago when Jeannie and I lived in Indiana while working in my parents' church, Jeannie got so frustrated with me (though neither of us now remember why) that she decided to get on a plane and head back to her family in Southern California. Storming out of the dining room and into the bedroom to pack, all she would need was an airline ticket, and she would be on her way.

Fortunately for both of us, we didn't have enough money to buy the plane ticket, and she was forced to stick with me and work it out. Thirty years later, we agree that what felt like bondage at the time turned out to be one of many bonding experiences for both of us.

Covenants will hold us together even when we are falling apart.

A healthy society is held together by covenants. Two of the most crucial cornerstones of covenant are money and marriage. In the following chapters, you will begin to understand the vital role those covenants play in your life and legacy. Your resources and relationships become the building blocks, and covenants become the cement that holds those blocks together for building a generational heritage.

What is a covenant, and how do we apply covenants in our lives?

Covenants Bring Bonding, Not Bondage

The quality of our lives is directly related to the quantity of covenants that we make. If we can see our relationships and resources as building blocks, then we must learn to use those blocks to build something of significance. By using the power of covenants, we can gather the people and possessions that God has blessed us with into the building of a lasting legacy.

Covenants may seem to be obligations that cramp your personal agenda or bring a pinch to your style. Often we fear that binding ourselves to something might cause us to miss something else just around the corner. Whether it is a commitment to a mate or a church community or even a job, we fear making that covenant. What if something better comes along?

The problem is that life can swiftly pass us by, leaving us on the corner waiting for the next big thing—that *something more* to satisfy the cravings that we have. Too many people end up living lives that are aloof and alone.

Covenants do not bring bondage. Bondage is found in the lonely heart of one who refuses to make a commitment. Bondage is living one's last years alone with only a pension check and a condo in some senior citizen complex. Bondage is the sparsely attended funeral service of a person who would not embrace the challenging adventures of relationships.

Bonding, on the other hand, brings a quality of life that helps us endure and even enjoy the sometimes painful process of living. Covenant is what forms the bond that connects you to legacy.

The Essential Elements of a Covenant

God is a covenant-making God. Everything God does is by, through, and because of covenant.

The Bible is a book of covenants. Specifically, the central focus of both the Old and New Testaments is centered on the covenant God made with Abraham and his descendants. This covenant is the foundation of the Christian faith.

Let's look at the essential elements of this covenant through Abraham. (See Genesis 12–15.) The first thing we discover is that Abraham was a Chaldean. He was not a Jew—there was no Jewish nation, and yet he became the father of the Jews.

How did this work?

Although the biological link was absent, the covenant God made with Abraham actually changed his DNA. God had *adopted* him into His family. This is why I believe that those who are adopted become grafted into a new lineage. Through the power of the covenant, a new DNA strand is fused into their bloodline. This mystical miracle happens by and through faith. Faith becomes the matrix (womb) where this new lineage is formed. Covenants are amazingly potent in their power. Enter into covenants carefully and soberly—but do enter!

That was just the beginning of God's miracles with Abraham's bloodline. God told him, "I'm going to start a whole new nation from you, and that nation will one day produce *the Seed* [Christ], and from that seed shall all nations be blessed." (See Genesis 17:1–22.)

Abraham said, "Say what?"

Abraham's wife, Sarah, was ninety years old. When he told her what God said, she laughed. She thought she was over the hill. She was sagging and wagging and tagging and just didn't feel like she had it in her.

Don't be discouraged about the challenges of building your legacy.

Christ grafted each of us into the tree of the same covenant. (See Romans 9.) Our covenant with Christ is directly connected to Abraham and the Jewish nation. Their place in history coincides with and confirms our faith.

Jesus taught that the Jewish nation would be a sign to Christians.

Two thousand years after Christ walked this earth, the Jewish nation and the same hundred-mile radius that Christ's ministry impacted are still the center of our world. Do you realize that the world's economy, energy (oil), and religions all revolve around this same territory on which Christ walked and talked? Their covenant—their blood—impacts our legacy.

In light of that, a study of the DNA of the Jewish people adds to this revelation concerning the power of the blood.

DNA carries two different types of cellular information: functional and historical.[1] Most of the material about DNA that we read is from the side of function, such as how the different cells influence whether or not a pigment gene causes blue or brown eyes, or their effect on character and charisma.

But DNA also carries historical data. By looking at a person's DNA it is possible to tell who that person's ancestors were and not only in the generations of recent history, which would include grandparents to great-great-grandparents. We can go back hundreds of generations.

According to studies, DNA analyses demonstrate that Jews all around the world—from the Middle East to the Midwest, from the Jewish ghettos of Europe to the villages of the sub-Saharan Africa, have preserved the same telltale pattern of DNA snippets. Despite the Diaspora, the Inquisition, and the Holocaust, Jews have sustained their genetic heritage as well as their religious traditions.[2]

> **A covenant is "a promise made with God as a witness."**

The coalescence of the DNA sequences can be dated to approximately three thousand years ago—the time of the exodus from Egypt, according to the Scriptures. Without a nation, a homeland for two thousand years, how could such a miraculous heritage be kept?

That's the power of a covenant. It holds people together when everything else is pulling them apart. So just what is a covenant? How do we engage with this awesome bonding?

FIVE ELEMENTS OF COVENANT

Let's use this story of Abraham to explore the five elements of a covenant.

Now the LORD had said to Abram:

"Get out of your country,
From your family
And from your father's house,
To a land that I will show you.

I will make you a great nation;
I will bless you and make your name great;
And you shall be a blessing.
I will bless those who bless you,
And I will curse him who curses you;
And in you all the families of the earth shall be blessed."
—GENESIS 12:1–3, EMPHASIS ADDED

1. Cause

All promises or covenants begin with a cause. Why and for what cause are you making a promise?

God told Abraham that He would bless him so that he would be a blessing. God intended to use Abraham as the means by which He would bless the human race. Abraham took ownership of his *blessing mantle.* He took the mantle on with a sense of responsibility.

Legacy can be simply understood as an organized way of blessing people for generations to come. It's nothing more (or less) than taking responsibility to assure that your relationships and resources will outlive and outlast your time on this earth. Do you have a sense of your calling? Have you tapped into the responsibility of the strengths and specific mandate on your lineage? "…who has saved us and called us with a holy calling, not according to our works, but according to His own purpose and grace which was given to us in Christ Jesus before time began" (2 Tim. 1:9).

How do you find that special cause and calling for your life?

I discovered a simple way to help you hone in on your passion and purpose. Ask yourself this question: "What makes me tick?" God has called you to a specific passion, and that passion is pounding in your heart right now. It's that one thing, that one activity, that causes you to lose track of time when you are engaged in it.

It's your gift. It's what you are graced to do, and it's what makes you glad. When you find what makes you tick, you are going to find the way to your holy calling. It's what I call your *passion pulse.*

Another question to ask is: "What makes me ticked?"

In other words, what makes you mad? Do you realize that your passion is linked to your pain? The word *passion* actually means, "the suffering, to be vexed." The pain and misery that you have experienced

117

will become the gain and ministry that God will use to fulfill your destiny. God does not waste a hurt. If you will identify the injustice and suffering that stirs you, then you can find the passion you need to find and fulfill your dream.

> **A legacy-driven life will produce more than it consumes.**

The final question is: "What "trickle-down" factors are in my lineage?" Search out your heritage. The clues for discovering and developing your destiny are in your DNA. If you will come under the influence of your generational attributes, you will confirm and conform to the plan that God had in mind for you before time began. Your purpose and the power to fulfill that purpose are in your DNA. It's called your passion power.

2. Commitment

The commitment would cost Abraham everything.

It seems contradictory for God to tell Abraham to leave his kin and country to begin a new family that would bless all the families of the earth.

Abram, as he was called before God established His covenant, was from a family of nomads. Nomads were people who roamed the land looking for resources that would meet their temporary needs for survival. After they exhausted the land's apparent resources, they would move on to other lands until again they used all the apparent resources.

Nomads were shortsighted and selfish. They were takers. There was never any thought of how they could establish a perpetual source from the land that would provide for them and for generations to come. They had a mentality of "take and take" until there was nothing more to take—no plowing, no pruning, and no preparing the ground for perpetual harvests to come. Abraham would change that way of thinking for everyone for all time.

Abraham was the first person ever recorded to buy land. People thought he was crazy! Why would anyone offer them money for land they did not own and that had already been stripped of all available resources?

Abraham taught us how to sow and reap and tap the unlimited resources of the land. He taught us that if you take care of the land, the land will take care of you. If you sow seeds for generations to come, the supply will be endless.

You and I were not put on this earth to be takers. Abraham broke through to a whole new way of living—legacy living!

In every generation there are those who must set in motion a new order. As we have mentioned before, Perez's name—the name of Tamar's son in the genealogy of Christ—in Hebrew means "the breaker." Every once in a while there comes a breakout person who must say, "I will leave the predicted and predictable path to begin a legacy that will break iniquity and bring forth equity for future generations." This requires commitment.

Legacy takes generations to reach its peak potential. An interesting insight of the Scriptures reveals that when a covenant lasts for three generations, a very special level of authority with God is obtained.

Something very dynamic occurs in the third-generation cycle of a legacy. Three is a number that speaks of wholeness. When a covenant is kept into the third generation, a perpetuated pattern manifests with a release of a distinguishable and determined force. Take note of families, churches, businesses, and even countries that have obtained the three-generation covenant cycle. It becomes an unstoppable force on the earth.

I call it *Generation³* (to the third power). That's why I believe the most powerful prayers in the Bible were prayed using the power of three.

"May the God of Abraham, Isaac, and Jacob…" is a common prayer tag used to gain authority with God in times of great need. When you have learned or earned the right to tag on your own three-generational deep covenant to your prayers, you are carrying what I call *covenant clout!*

The first generation is characterized by the *sacrifice* that someone must plow for a legacy to get on the right track. Most of the efforts of that generation end up being the plowing and sowing that will not be reaped until the second generation. The second generation, as a result, will experience the reaping of much success. Success should be received as being more of a responsibility than a reward. The harvest will bring its own share of strain and will require sacrificial strategic labor in order for the success to be sustained. The crucial transition of a legacy will be in taking the sacrifice and successful efforts of one generation and seeing them passed on to the next. The *succession* of the legacy becomes the real test of the success and sacrifice of the first two generations.

When the third generation has properly received the baton and the succession is complete, an exponential leap of a legacy occurs. Abraham had one covenant son, Isaac. Isaac had two sons, and Jacob had twelve sons. From those twelve sons of Jacob, all the tribes of Israel are named.

By the fourth generation, the legacy will be well on its way in establishing *significance*. A New Testament example is found in the testimony of Timothy: "When I call to remembrance the genuine faith that is in you, which dwelt first in your *grandmother* Lois and your *mother* Eunice, and I am persuaded is in *you* also" (2 Tim. 1:5, emphasis added).

Timothy, the young bishop of the first-century church, was a third-generation legacy link. That's the level you want to get to.

If you want to establish a Timothy legacy, it starts with godly grandparents. There are no shortcuts to legacy. Whatever it takes to get a successful third-generation link will be worth it. Someone once said that it takes a hundred years to raise a great child. That's legacy thinking.

The story of Timothy shows that a single mom (or father) can build a legacy. Remember that the blessing that sanctifies the children requires only one believing parent (1 Cor. 7:14). Stay committed to your principles and dreams. Know that God is with you and will be there for you no matter what your circumstances. You *will* have a godly legacy.

3. Confirmation

Legacy is the perpetuation of a blessing. The blessing is the unique favor that can and should be passed from one generation to another. A blessing requires three things: the actual *blessing*, which is the initial cause; the *blesser*, the one who gives the blessing; and then, of course, the *blessee*, the one who receives the blessing.

The covenant we make is the moral instrument that *protects* and *projects* that blessing. Only some person or some institution with authority can establish a covenant.

A legacy has authority only to the degree that it is under authority. A legacy is not made unto one's self, neither can it be on one's authority.

Just as you need a legal instrument and agency to recognize a legal will, so, spiritually, you must have a relationship with those whom God has given you as His agents and instruments to confirm your covenant. (See Hebrews 13:7, 17.)

When Abraham was given the opportunity to show that he was submitted to the authority of God, he did so with unwavering and quick obedience. The tithe that was paid to Melchizedek proved the accountability that Abraham had to God (Gen. 14:18–24).

A legacy cannot be established without being a part of a covenant community. That's why I am a firm believer in the local church as the authority that can recognize and provide the support that it takes to build a legacy.

A church is more than a mission, more than a charitable cause. The church is the authority of God on the earth. It brings accountability and access to the relationships and resources that will be at work long after we're gone: "…how you ought to conduct yourself in the house of God, which is the church of the living God, the pillar and ground of the truth" (1 Tim. 3:15).

Without the church, our covenants can become nothing more than legalese or even loose agreements that have no true spiritual covenant connection. The church that you are in covenant with legitimizes all other covenants. Think about it. The marriage certificate is only as good as the institution in which it is recognized. The giving of our time and treasures to our local church gives or takes away the credibility of the covenants we make. Upon what authority do you make your promises? Who or what stands behind your covenants? If you are dealing with someone who is a believer and yet has no accountability to God through a Bible-based church, you have a contract, not a covenant. If a person feels no sense of obligation to God with his or her motives, money, or marriage, how are they going to have the conviction to keep a promise made to you or me?

It's no wonder that it takes a stack of papers thicker than the Bible, along with a dozen lawyers, to keep our relationships and resources from being exploited. (See 1 Corinthians 6.)

4. Conflict

We will all face the temptation to break our promises. It can be easy to make a promise with our lips, but every promise will face conflict.

Our covenants carry no weight until they pass through conflict. Your promise has no credibility until you have faced the pain and pressure of holding on to your vow in the midst of adversity. Adversity will introduce you to your legacy.

When Abraham made a sacrifice to God to establish the covenant, God asked him to take an animal and cut it in two pieces. Then God and Abraham walked between the sacrifices, together, making a promise. It's as if they were saying, "May we be torn apart before we would tear this promise apart. May we be broken before we would break this vow." That's the commitment you will need to have in order to face and overcome the conflict from a covenant!

Covenant is a promise made with God as your witness. It's not always easy to make or keep.

After four years of intense labor in our desire to plant Life Church, Jeannie and I became painfully aware that we were not building the fastest-growing church in the world. There was nothing "fast" about anything we were doing except our fast-depleting funds. Every time we thought we were turning the corner, we hit another wall. We went from a couple hundred people down to a handful. We lost the building we were renting and had to use another church on Sunday afternoons.

Conflict transforms our convictions into covenants.

In a sincere attempt to help us, my friends and family began sharing ministry opportunities that were available across the country. At first it was interesting to hear of the many churches that offered facilities and a core of dedicated members. But it soon became an irritation to my spirit.

After a depressing weekend, I received a call with an impressive opportunity. I should have been intrigued, but instead I felt upset. I told them, "You are asking me to commit spiritual adultery! Don't insult the commitment and calling we have to this region."

One of the greatest lessons God taught me during that season was, "If you take failure personally, you will take success personally." My commitment was and is based upon my obedience to God. So it is with a legacy; it does not come by casual desire. It requires the desire of the passionate and the courage of the strong.

Are you the first in your known lineage to step into the land of opportunity for a life lived beyond you and now? If so, may God grant you the grace to stand on your promise—so help you God! Count it all joy to enter into your time of testing. It reveals the true you to yourself. Let conflict expose and eliminate any weak areas of your commitment. Turn your test into your testimony.

During my brother-in-law's training camp, when he was becoming a U.S. Marine, he became exhausted to the point that he felt like he was going to pass out while running. There would be no sympathy.

"Coffey," the sergeant shouted out his name. "Do you know what weakness is?"

"Sir, no sir," Nathan responded back.

"Weakness is pain leaving your body."

Sometimes, conflict is nothing more than that. Covenant will need all your might and strength to endure. Don't be afraid to face conflict. It's all part of the covenant process.

5. Continuum

The most important aspect of a covenant is the responsibility to see it continue to the next generation. No matter how noble the cause and your personal commitment to that cause, if it is not passed successfully to the next generation, all you have done will be for naught. "I will establish my covenant as an everlasting covenant between me and you and your descendants after you for the generations to come, to be your God and the God of your descendants after you" (Gen. 17:7, NIV).

Late one evening, D. L. Moody, the premier American evangelist of the 1800s, arrived home from speaking at a meeting. Emma, his wife, was already asleep. As her exhausted husband climbed into bed, she rolled over and murmured, "So how did it go?"

"Pretty well," he replied. "Two and a half converts."

His wife lay silently for a moment pondering this response, then she finally smiled. "That's sweet." Then she said, "How old was the child?"

"No, no, no," Moody answered. "It was two children and one adult. The children have their whole lives in front of them. The adult's life is already half gone."[3]

Most of us would think like D. L. Moody's wife—the children are often considered only half as important as adults. Our covenants are in grave danger because of that mind-set.

Understanding the covenant plans that God has for them is crucial for our children to grasp. It seems so obvious—teach your children well so they can tell their children and their children's children. Yet, we are failing to do so. Everything that God does for and through us could be lost in one generation. A country or a church could lose its way simply by not securing the virtues and values from one generation to another.

> **Nothing matters if it does not get passed on to the next generation.**

Every day you and I must be reminded of the responsibility we have for showing our children the principles of God's Word, which we have been taught—and not just our children, but also all the children. Keep your eyes and heart open for every opportunity to teach a child. Volunteer at a church or school. Look out for the fatherless or even the single-father households. Every one of us is a player in this awesome task of perpetuating the covenants that we have been so graciously given.

These five principles become the foundation and framework of what a covenant is. These truths will establish and sustain your legacy.

HOMEMADE EQUITY

How does a covenant work?

In very simple terms, it's like when we buy a house—we either pay cash for it or we *covenant* with a financial institute for the money to buy the property. This usually requires a down payment and a binding contract that itemizes the terms of the loan. With enough of your own money or assets on the line, the bank is secure enough to loan you the money.

After you take possession, you begin to build equity in your home. If you live in Southern California like we do, a $600,000 home (which is the median price today) could potentially bring a $300,000–$600,000 increase in equity in ten years. Wow!

Of course, during that time you may have plumbing problems, furnace problems, or other repairs that stretch you beyond your budget. We have had times when we had to scratch and strain to find the cash to fix a problem in our home.

Was it hard? Did it cause us discomfort and distress? Yes. There were times when it would have been easier just to be a renter and call the landlord when there was a problem. Let the landlord worry about it; I'll kick back and go out for a steak dinner!

But what would I have after renting for ten years? Nothing!

How many equity-building covenants do you have in your life? Are you *renting* your relationships? Do you *lease* your church community? How long will you just get by with the least amount of commitment to the relationships and resources that God has placed in your life?

That should make you think about just how many covenants you may or may not have. But there are more good things to learn about the covenant life.

BINDING CONTRACT

> Whatever you bind on earth will be bound in heaven, and whatever you loose on earth will be loosed in heaven. Again I say to you that if two of you agree on earth concerning anything that they ask, it will be done for them by My Father in heaven.
>
> —MATTHEW 18:18–19

Covenants strengthen you. They create a power and a force.

When you make promises with God as your witness, you are binding God's strength into your life. The more covenants you have, the more vehicles God has to empower your life. Once you understand the power of covenants, you will be chasing them to see how many you can make.

The reason we lack power over the devil is not the fault of our Holy Spirit connection. The Scriptures declare, "Greater is he that is in you, than he that is in the world" (1 John 4:4, KJV), but if that is the case, why, then, are so many of us getting beat up and beat down?

It's the lack of covenant making that has weakened our authority.

The word *oath* (another word for *covenant*) in the Greek means "to bind or attach," and it comes from the word *exorcism*. With a covenant, you bind something to you, and you oath out (exorcise) the enemy. Covenants bind God's promises to you, and they bind Satan's power from you. You bind the devil by the authority you stand in, based upon the covenants that you have made.

Where an oath or a covenant is established, Satan has no authority.

On the other hand, what is not in covenant is Satan's to mess with. Without a covenant, the devil gains access illegally to your "stuff."

Jesus taught about how the devil works in our generation in the twelfth chapter of Matthew. Even after being cast out by the strongman, the devil remained unconvinced until a binding covenant had been made. The devil returns and says, "I will return to my house from which I came" (Matt. 12:44). He thinks he is welcome in your house. He is a liar, a moocher, and a squatter. He thinks that your house is his house and your children are his children.

There is a system of the world that is out to kill, steal, and destroy your legacy. This system works against God and righteousness. For example, you may be watching television or a movie. The sun is setting, and the violins are playing, and some guy is about to begin an adulterous affair. They set it up in such a way that tears cloud your eyes, and you think, "Oh, this just feels so right. This man deserves love."

You have just been drawn into a very hurtful, damaging event. You have become an ally with the principality that causes sin, destroys marriages, hurts children and communities, and grieves the heart of God. There is nothing good in an adulterous affair—I don't care how lovely the music sounds. When it really happens, there is no violin playing. However, there is a lot of pain playing out in the lives of many people.

You should be thinking, "You know what? This isn't right. This is simply not right."

Sometimes entertainment feels more like innerTAINTment! You must confront the worldly system and loose it from your life. You must choose that which is right and bind it to your life. If you're going to have binding and loosening ability, you must live according to the Word and not according to the world.

Bind yourself to the ways and life of Jesus. Jesus was the perfect man. He lived the perfect life. You and I get to have the perfect relationship with the Father because of the perfect blood of Christ. Never mind your sinful past, redemption has given you a bright future. It's in the DNA you have through faith in Christ.

TAKING AUTHORITY: ENFORCE THE FORCE

We are like policemen who have been given the authority to enforce the laws of the land. We don't make the laws; we just put the laws into effect.

It's not your power. It's not your works or words. You are simply executing the authority of Christ and His Word. If you are in covenant with God and you know the law of God's Word, your words carry the authority of God. We are truly in a *war of words*. It's His Word against the enemy's words.

But don't think that the enemy will let up easily. The devil is counting on you to live by the *selfish gene* you have entered this life with and passively forfeit your legacy.

Legacy is a battlefield. You are a warrior in this war.

Warriors fight for causes that are bigger than their individual lives. The thought that they may lose their lives for the principle at stake is a cost they have counted. What pounds in the heart of a true warrior is the benefits others will receive from the potential loss of their life.

When you pray to take authority over the enemy, don't expect him to say, "Aw, shucks. Man, I wish you wouldn't have prayed that. See you later." Oh, no! On his way out, he will be screaming and kicking.

If you don't know how to hold on to your faith, you might give up your victory. You might allow yourself to let go of what God has put in your hands. Have faith. Have confidence in the unseen.

A new Christian had a dream. In the dream she heard a sound in her living room and went to see what the commotion was. She came upon a disturbing creature that was stealing her valuable possessions and putting them in a bag. "I rebuke you in the name of Jesus," she declared. The foul creature mocked her, saying, "I'm not afraid of that name."

Not knowing what else to do, she kept rebuking him. This time she noticed that, although the devilish creature continued to say he was not afraid of that name, he was taking all the items out of the bag and putting them back, running out of the house all the while yelling, "I'm not afraid of that name!"

Satan is a liar and a sore loser. Even when defeated, he will not acknowledge the truth. Stand your ground, and you will see the victory manifested in your life.

We are in a war over—you guessed it—our seed. The enemy's number one goal is to stop your legacy. The battle over your heirs is intensified when you realize that because the devil is a fallen angel—and angels cannot reproduce—his only means of extending his perverted *legacy* is through our children. The imagery of this battle is described in dramatic fashion in the twelfth chapter of the Book of Revelation. (See Revelation 12:4, 11, 17.) We know who wins, and we know how the battle is won. It is through the Word of the Lord, which becomes your tested word, and the power of the blood of Jesus.

Stand and stay the course of God's Word. Don't give up and don't give in. There is no greater covenant than what we have in the Holy Scriptures.

Psalm 15 gives instruction for those who want to have access to God. It says they keep their oath even when it hurts. "LORD, who may abide in Your tabernacle?...He who swears to his own hurt and does not change" (vv. 1, 4).

In other words, you'll break me before I'll break this oath. That's the power you have when you make an oath. You know it's going to work because the covenant is more important than your feelings at any given moment.

A covenant brings out the best in you. You will come to know yourself; more importantly, you will own yourself. There is a deep joy that results from enduring the struggles to keep your commitment to the covenant. There is real fulfillment in having "stuck to it" and stayed the course, and knowing that your word is your bond.

THE FINISH LINE

The 1968 Mexico City Olympics produced the story about the "Last Man in the Marathon." A little more than an hour after the winner had crossed the finish line, with only a few thousand spectators left in the stadium, the last runner finally arrived. With a leg bandaged and bloody, he made his painful way around the last lap.

A columnist wrote, "Today we have seen a young African runner who symbolizes the finest in the human spirit... [in a] performance that gives true meaning to sport... a performance that lifts sport out of the category of grown men playing games... a performance that gives meaning to the word courage.... All honor to John Stephen Akhwari of Tanzania."[4]

Afterward Akhwari was asked why he had endured the pain since there was no chance of winning. He simply said, "My country did not send me to Mexico City to start the race. They sent me to finish."[5]

Covenant people understand that finishing what you start is the name of the game. Run with integrity. Finish with intensity. Own your oath.

> **Character becomes your destiny. Character is what it takes to build an enduring legacy.**

You can only give what you own. You can only serve with that which you have first mastered. A broken person will break his or her word. A wounded heart cannot endure hardship. A person must leave himself before he can leave a covenant relationship. When you lose your own worth, it will manifest in the way you lack the courage and stamina to sustain your promises. It takes a strong person to make a covenant. It takes an even stronger person to keep it. Difficulties will not destroy a covenant; they actually serve to develop character.

CHAPTER 9

Marriage: Why Knot?
Marriage gets its groove back

A man leaves his father and mother and is joined to his wife,
and the two are united into one.

—Ephesians 5:31, nlt

EVERY GREAT LEGACY IN THE BIBLE RESULTED FROM A COMMITTED marriage: Abraham and Sarah, Isaac and Rebekah, Jacob and Rachel, David and Bathsheba, Jesus and the church.

There are two covenants that are the cornerstone of every society—marriage and money. When these covenants are broken, all other covenants are at risk.

Let's begin with marriage.

If you are single, please don't skip this chapter. What you are about to read will change you and prepare you for how you view the covenant of marriage. The next few minutes will be defining moments for your legacy.

Marriage is the covenant of covenants. It sets the standard for all covenants. If a culture has a difficult time supporting the marriage covenant, it will struggle with all covenants.

How did we lose the covenant and celebration of marriage? How did marriage lose its groove?

If marriage was a stock, its value would have dropped to the loss column of our culture's portfolio. It is almost as if there is a conspiracy against it. If you check the statistics of those living together and of people divorced and staying unmarried, you get a picture of a society that seems to be shunning the institution of marriage.

Even in the Christian community, we are struggling to hold our vows intact, with divorce rates nearly the same as in the secular community. Our antimarriage culture is resisting God's plan and purpose. We need to reestablish God's laws of family. Marriage is a sacred and holy commitment that holds a culture together. That one little piece of paper does matter. The vows we make in public with the recognition of the church are not just a good thing—they are a God thing.

What is the worth of a promise made with God as a witness?

When you lock into a covenant, God says, "I'll help you. You make Me the witness; I'll give you My help." When you enter the covenant of marriage, God says, "All right. I'll give you the power to keep that."

So it's right to say, "As God is my witness—so help me God."

The real vow is not what you say to each other. The real vow is the vow to the marriage and to the covenant. You and your love are along for the ride of your life. This wonderful institution is bigger and more vital than even your love for each other.

When you can't believe in the marriage, believe in the covenant of that marriage. If you are having marital problems but are committed to a strong covenant, the covenant will get you through the bad times.

Now, this is counter to the current culture. Our culture says, "Hey, I want to be free." Marriage is looked on as a burden. It's what you do as a last resort after all your other options are explored and exhausted: "I've finished college, I've dated everyone, I've been to Europe, I'm getting tired and losing some hair, so now I'll get married."

We need to have this kind of mind-set: "I'll thrive; I'll be more successful with a helpmate."

> Because the LORD has been witness
> Between you and the wife of your youth,
> With whom you have dealt treacherously;
> Yet *she is your companion*
> *And your wife by covenant.*
> But did He *not make them one,*
> Having a remnant of the Spirit?
> And why one?

He seeks godly offspring....
For the LORD God...hates divorce,
For it covers one's garment with violence.
                    —MALACHI 2:14–16, EMPHASIS ADDED

New surveys are demonstrating what the Scriptures teach. A study by Pew Research Center found that married people are nearly twice as happy as those who are not married. Regular churchgoers—those who attend at least once a week—are nearly twice as happy than those who seldom or never attend.[1] You should be a very jolly creature if you are married and going to church!

So many people today are living together. When I counsel them, they say, "I want to be sure." If you're not sure—get sure! Move out until you are sure. The Bible says, "Marriage is honorable among all, and the bed undefiled" (Heb. 13:4). In other words, the bed is a sanctuary of celebration that is rightfully given to those in marriage.

The patent for marriage belongs to God. He created it, and He owns the rights. Marriage was made in the image of His relationship with you and me. (See Ephesians 5:23–32.)

God could sue some for patent infringement! We don't have the right to take marital privileges and use them unless we have been obedient to the owner's manual. We can't tinker with God's institutions.

God made man, and then God created woman from man, and the one became two. The Bible says that the two become one again through the marriage institution and physical intimacy.

The Scriptures teach that when you have sexual intimacy, you become one with that person. It's not just a biological exchange—it's a spiritual event. (See 1 Corinthians 6:16–20; 7:1–40.)

Sex is a beautiful and powerful expression of a promise that has been made. The promise is that two souls have been joined into one flesh, and they cannot be separated. Sex is the exchanging of DNA. There is nothing casual about it. "For this cause shall a man leave father and mother, and shall cleave to his wife: and they twain shall be one flesh" (Matt. 19:5, KJV).

For this cause, a man shall leave to cleave. The Greek definition of *cleave* is "to adhere to," so I think of glue. You shall be glued. You know the rules for glue. They're real easy. The label says, "Apply to clean surface." Then, once attached, do not pull off. The glue loses effectiveness if you keep pulling it off and attaching it somewhere else.

If you reapply this bonding power time after time, when you finally find the right person you will have lost the bond that God created to keep your marriage together.

This *glue* will hold you together when everything else is falling apart, even through wavering emotions, conflicting opinions, and the stress of life. The urge to merge will work. God has given us tools to help keep our covenants.

The covenant in itself contains the power to keep the covenant. Know that God will give you what you need to live out what He wants you to live in. As my dear friend Dr. Jim Reeve says, "You make the choices; God will make the changes."

THE HOLY UNION OF MARRIAGE AND LEGACY

Families hold societies together. In Adam Bellow's book I*n Praise of Nepotism: A Natural History*, he claims: "All civilizations survive on three basic activities: 1) to marry; 2) to reproduce; 3) to leave a heritage."[2] When those simple elements are violated or ignored, a civil order of life cannot—will not—exist. All society is based upon the cornerstone of marriage. When you start undermining this cornerstone—for example, separating reproduction from marriage—you begin breaking down society.

If God has called you to be single like the apostle Paul, be a supporter of marriage in every way possible. We support those who go to college to become doctors, lawyers, and teachers. In the same way, we must support those who are committed to marriage. Do the homework. If we as a society do not make our homes work, will anything else we do matter?

Do we even understand how a society's relational economy works? We are undermining our civil order with the slothful handling of the covenant of marriage. It's not an exaggeration to say that our future is built on that little piece of paper called the *marriage certificate*.

Legacy is linked to the covenant of marriage, reproduction (children by birth or adoption), and the leaving of a heritage (and the wholehearted support of those who cannot marry or have children).

I have been greatly influenced by Adam Bellow's book on nepotism.

It has helped me to articulate the vital role of family transferring responsibilities and rewards.

The modern definition of *nepotism* is "favoritism based on kinship." When understood, it may very well be the single most important attribute this culture has for survival.

Sure, we all know bad nepotism when we see it, but it is a fact that bad nepotism is its own judgment. Like a man who was born on third base and thinks he hit a triple, without eventually earning the right to one's heritage, failure will come quickly and furiously.

The desire to give your children a legacy is a God-given impulse.

This is the way we pass on our values and beliefs. Without this link, the human race will not survive. It is our biological bytes that program us to transfer the principles we have learned and earned to our seed. Encoded in the tension of godly nepotism is a moral accountability that cannot be replicated by law or social leverage. Nepotism is the healthy practice of a generational-driven culture.

Don't be ashamed or intimidated of the blessings you have been given by your forefathers. Build on them, and become a force that forms a positive society that will have lasting influence.

Our economical strength as a country is a testimony of good nepotism. About 95 percent of all American businesses are still family owned or controlled, including about 40 percent of Fortune 500 companies.

It has become an enjoyable obsession for me to match successful people to their DNA. From pastors, actors, politicians, artists, and enterprisers, the DNA transfer is staggering and stimulating to the practice of value-based nepotism. Nepotism is another way of making a covenant with your family to carry on for the next generation.

God uses love and marriage as a cornerstone for legacy. He brings exactly the right two people together to create the next generation He needs to fulfill His plans.

One of the sure ways to ensure that your marriage is of God is to observe the differences between you and your mate. It's good

Every covenant matters!

genetic management—a little bit of this and a little bit of that, and you have a child who has what it takes to succeed and add significance to your legacy.

Covenants are indeed the mortar that holds the relationships and resources of our lives together. The quality of our life is determined by the quantity of those covenants we make.

THE YOUNG AND THE RESTLESS

Claude Levi-Strauss was an anthropologist who went to the jungle in central Brazil. He saw that everybody was together, laughing and eating. Then he noticed a man who was always alone and looked weak and depressed. He asked, "What's wrong with him? Does he have a disease?"

And they said, "Oh, no. He's a bachelor."[3] Throughout history, being a bachelor has not been celebrated as an achievement or a status to be celebrated.

According to the results of the Census Bureau's American Community Survey 2005, more American women fifteen and older are living without a husband than with one for the first time in U.S. history. It's reported that 51 percent of women are living without a spouse, up from 35 percent in 1950.[4] There are several factors for this sharp rise, including living together and waiting longer to be married after a death or divorce. This is not good news for our culture. The cornerstone for legacy is built on relationships and marriage in particular. As our society tears away at this foundation, we will weaken our ability to sustain the significance that can only be perpetuated by covenantal commitments.

The chain of events that start in one *single* decision affects all of us.

How? For starters, the gap widens between child and grandparents (almost to a place of little or nonexistent relationship). This social problem is sneaking up on us. Those who wait to get married and have children add yet another year that the grandparents will not be involved in the life of the next generation. (I am very much aware that for some, when or if they will have a child is not their choice. Grace to you; God will show you how you too can have a legacy.) For others, their willful choice to not have or to delay having children could be a subtle eroding of the family tree that will take a generation or two to feel its effect. Read this disturbing prophetic word from the prophet Samuel: "But now the LORD says: '...so that there will not be an old man in your house...despite all the good which God does for Israel. And there shall not be an old man in your house forever'" (1 Sam. 2:30–32).

I will walk carefully through the minefield of the complexities of challenges you may be facing in your relationships that cannot be resolved by one-line dogmas. But nonetheless, it must be said: Marriage is more of a moral responsibility than a monetary reward. Marriage is a call to become holy—not just happy! Marriage should be desired, not despised.

We may have set a standard for qualifying for marriage that may be unreasonable and also destructive to the success God has planned for our youth. We discourage our young adults from getting married until they "get it all together" educationally and financially and become more stable. Do we think marriage will slow them down or impede their progress?

We are sending a message to our youth that says marriage is a liability. We have *sold* marriage as a problem rather than a solution. Think about the dilemma we place them in. We are asking them to be sexually inactive during the ages of eighteen to thirty—years when their hormones peak in a biological effort to insure reproduction. They believe our words of caution because our own shaky marriages send a message that this institution may be a bad investment.

Marriage is not a liability; it is an asset! Two are better than one. Marriage, though it is indeed a challenging journey, is the destiny for most of us. Within reason, the sooner we can get started, the better. It would not be unreasonable to help a young couple financially if needed. Why should we punish our children by cutting them off financially because they choose to marry?

The old children's song says:

> Phil and Jeannie sitting in a tree, k-i-s-s-i-n-g,
> First comes love, then comes marriage,
> Then comes a baby in a baby carriage.

This song may seem to have lost its present pop culture relevance, but it describes best what love is all about from God's perspective.

When I married Jeannie, I was about as immature as you can be. The day of our wedding, I called Jeannie in a panic and asked her how I was to pack. Other than the money we received in cards from our church and family, we had nothing. Dumb? Maybe. Wrong? Maybe not!

The question we should ask about marriage is, what is important to God? Is it economic stability? Are long engagements and extended periods of testing compatibility important?

As unromantic as it may sound, the solution for a young person's issue with sex and sloth, according to the Scriptures, could be the commitment of marriage—not just vows of purity, classes on abstinence, or instructions to "rebuke the devil." The solution is quite straightforward: let him find a wife!

I have people come to me and say, "I'm burning with passion. I want to be physically involved with somebody. Lay hands on me so I can be delivered from this strong desire." You know what the Bible says to do when you're burning with passion? The Bible says that if you're burning, get married (1 Cor 7:9). When I tell them this, they say, "Oh, but I don't want to get married because then I'll be bound, and I want to be free."

Freedom is what you feel when you are doing what is right. Every day you're not building covenants in your relationships and/or your resources, you are weakening your life's influence. Embrace the covenant life.

HAPPY AND HOLY

Marriage isn't just about being happy. It's so much more meaningful than that. It's about being holy. Marriage is a *holy* place that will make us *wholly* whole when we are under its covenant covering. If you really understand why God wants you to be married, you will understand how to be successful at it. If you understand the responsibility of being holy, you can truly enjoy the reward of being happy.

Anyone who knows Jeannie and me are aware that we are the best of friends and that we enjoy a full and fulfilled married life. We experience both the happiness and the holiness that comes with the covenant of marriage.

Having said that and assured myself a chance at some more happy moments in my marriage, we must grow past the fantasy that marriage is about sharing a life of romantic dreams every day of your life. Marriage can be tough, and you may even find yourself looking for the escape latch during certain seasons of your marriage. You will actually have more happiness in your marriage when you see that your *wholly-ness* is the number one objective in a covenant relationship. Legacy and longevity form the alliance that will simply outlast any passing problems you think are not bearable when taking your issues too personally and failing to see the generational and eternal benefits of a covenant.

Dietrich Bonhoeffer said:

> Marriage is more than your love for each other. It has a higher dignity and power, for it is God's holy ordinance, through which he wills to perpetuate the human race till the end of time. In your love you see only two selves in the world, but in marriage you are a link in the chain of the generations.... In your love, you see only the heaven of your own happiness, but in marriage you are placed at a post of responsibility toward the world and mankind. Your love is your own private possession, but marriage is more than something personal—it is a status, an office. Just as it is the crown, and not merely the will to rule, that makes the king, so it is marriage, and not merely your love for each other, that joins you together in the sight of God and man. As high as God is above man, so high are the sanctity, the rights, and the promise of marriage above the sanctity, the rights, and the promise of love. It's not your love that sustains the marriage, but the marriage that sustains your love.[5]

You ask, "Should a husband and wife stay together for the children's sake if they're having a rough time?" Absolutely! With the exceptions of abuse, abandonment, or adultery, your covenant is more important than your convenience.

"But I'm not happy," you say. Well, you can work on that. Get a hobby. Get therapy. Do something. Find a way to get happy. But don't break the covenant.

How much legacy equity is in a ten-, twenty-, or thirty-year marriage? How would you calculate the worth of having a mom and dad present, sitting side by side at their child's high school graduation, wedding, or the birth of their children's children? Price that out. Next time you are feeling sad or depressed about how unhappy you are with the ways of your mate, compare the price of your emotions against the emotions of your children and their children as they deal with the negative force of divorce.

Maybe, just maybe, you can work through your issues and find a way to work through and not walk from the priceless worth of a covenant marriage.

I was at a store one day, and a little boy got on the cell phone and said, "Mom? I'm going to buy a snowboard, but I won't be bringing it home. I'm going to leave it at Dad's house."

It took me a few minutes to figure it out. You see—I woke up every morning to my mother and my father in the same house. I've lived with one woman all my life. I don't understand what it would be like to wake up and realize that my father is not here, or my mother is not here, and that I go back and forth. At that moment my heart just ached, and I said, "God, give us a generation that would say, 'By God's grace, if I bring a child into this world, I'll bring it by covenant, and I'll keep that covenant.'"

God said, "Don't leave. I brought the two of you together because I want offspring to carry a mantle of favor." When the marriage covenant is broken, violence comes in and attempts to destroy the legacy that God is building through obedience.

Covenants are built on obedience.

Covenant is the currency of heaven. All exchanges of the heavenly assets come to us through the covenants we are willing to enter into.

The satisfaction is in the commitment we make and the fruit of a covenant kept.

What if you have gone through a divorce? What now?

For those who have gone through a divorce, thank you for letting me fight for marriages without you feeling more pain than you have already endured. I believe we should have conviction without condemnation.

One of my friends who went through a divorce told me that he now understands why God hates divorce. It is very difficult. Anyone who has gone through this *dividing force* knows that to be true. Divorce is often another problem and not a solution. There are scriptural grounds for getting a divorce, but my advice is to keep in mind that the rewards of a legacy will outlast any benefits of a divorce. Yes, you can have a legacy though divorced. It may require more work, but you can and will be of those who by God's grace make good out of the bad.

A MATCH WAITING TO SPARK

Paul and Toni lived on different continents ten thousand miles apart. They are an example of what God can do that would be impossible for us to do ourselves.

Toni is a South African woman who had gone through a painful divorce. In addition to losing her marriage, she lost her church family and her livelihood working at the church. She had her dog, her clothes, and a Christian couple who were both friends and mentors. That's it.

Toni spent three years in this place of brokenness and healing. At a time when she was feeling her lowest and believing that God had forsaken her because of her divorce, the Lord reached down with His long arms of mercy and poured out His grace on her like a soft cleansing rain. For three days she felt this tangible outpouring of His grace upon her. The love she felt that day still touches her every time she tells this part of her story, and she still gets all choked up in awe of His grace. She is so grateful for His grace and says that without that she would not be here today doing the work of the Lord.

During this period, Toni read a book called *God Is a Matchmaker*, by Derek Prince.[6] He tells the story of spending three years in the desert with the Bible as his only source of strength and courage. At the end of that period, God led him to the woman who would become his wife and helpmeet in a mission to help orphaned children in Jerusalem. Derek Prince offers a specific road map on how to trust God to prepare you and lead you to the mate He is preparing for you.

In this book, the story of Rebekah and how she left everything that was familiar to her—family, friends, and her country—to be joined to her groom, Isaac, was branded in Toni's heart. She felt that the Lord was raising her as the bride for her groom and that He was going to present her to her groom and that she too was going to live in a foreign land.

One night Toni was helping her friends host a couple from California. Hal Ezell was the former commissioner of immigration, and his wife, Lee Ezell, was a prominent public speaker. Five minutes after meeting Toni he said, "When are you coming to America? I have a husband for you!"

"Where?" she asked.

"In California."

Hal later sent her a picture of Paul, and she placed it in her Bible. Several months later when she picked up her Bible, the picture fluttered to the floor…face up. She immediately understood that she was to pray for Paul, and she was to pray specifically for his career.

Paul had been a single dad with custody of his children for ten years. During that time he had been introduced to many ladies, but he never felt that he had found the one. He was lonely, but he waited.

Meanwhile, after visiting the United States, where they were introduced to Paul, another couple returned home with a good report for Toni, saying: "We have met Paul. We know what kind of person he is. We know that he is the right one for you!"

Toni took this as a word from the Lord and the confirmation she was praying for. However, God would have to make a way for them to meet.

Shortly after Toni started praying for him, Paul got a significant promotion. The miracle had begun. Back in South Africa, Toni discovered a remarkable offer for a vacation in California where she would be introduced to Paul. The miracle was at hand.

At the end of her two-week vacation, the miracle fast-forwarded— Paul proposed! Today, Paul and Toni are serving ministries that include establishing homes in South Africa for abandoned AIDS babies. As a couple, they represent a true team and are a living testimony of what faith and faithfulness will bring to our lives.[7]

Marriage is not the *problem* in our society; it is the *solution*. The sooner we recapture this holy institute and support it through every means possible, the sooner we can enrich our culture, church, and country.

CHAPTER 10

Blood, Sweat, and Tears
Money grows on trees—family trees!

Your treasure is not just for pleasure. Rather, it is for leaving a legacy. Leaving the world better than you found it is not just your right—it's your responsibility.

LEGACIES ARE BUILT ON COVENANTS. COVENANTS ARE FOR THE success and succession of our relationships and resources. Both deal with the matters of the heart. Money is a clear indicator of our heart's motives.

There are two things about money that you need to understand. First, God wants you to be blessed. Second, the purpose is so you can be a blessing. But to truly come to a proper understanding of money matters, you must be committed to one very crucial principle...

When Jeannie and I were in our younger days of ministry, we toured the country speaking at youth conferences, special meetings, and church services. We had two kids at that time, and like many young couples, we were broke. We were worse than broke; we had run up about three thousand dollars in credit card debt and other bills. (That was in the early eighties.)

One Friday morning, Jeannie came to me and said, "Phil, we've got to stop this spending and pay off these bills." We both felt convicted. We knelt down and prayed for God to help us. We wisely cut up our credit cards and then in faith wrote out checks for the amounts due and put them in the return envelopes to be mailed when we had the money in our account.

Later that day, I was putting some mail in a drop box and I inadvertently put the credit card envelopes in with the rest of the mail, which meant that our checks were on their way to the credit card company, and there was no money in our account to cover them. Talk about panic.

Now we were going to incur extra fees from the credit card companies and our banks for writing rubber checks—not to mention the dings to our credit.

The following Sunday, a new convert from the church, a dentist, took us out to dinner. After dinner, as we were walking to our car, he said, "Hey, I felt impressed to give you guys something." And he handed me an envelope. I thanked him but told him that if it was money I couldn't take it. He would have to give it to the church where we were preaching, because they were responsible for paying us. He assured us that he had already talked to the pastor and told him that he would be doing this. Grateful for his generosity, I accepted the envelope.

"Oh, by the way," he said, "it's a blank check. Fill it out for whatever amount you need. As I was praying this past Friday morning the Lord put you both on my heart. Don't worry about the amount. It's not mine; it's God's money. I don't care if you fill it in for one hundred dollars or ten thousand dollars. God's just using my checking account to get it to you."

> One of the greatest missing teachings in the American church today is the reminder to men and women that nothing we have belongs to us.[1]
>
> —Gordon MacDonald

Jeannie and I were stunned. We called the pastor of the church and asked him what we should do. "Do what the man told you," he said. So we did. We paid our debt, paid our tithes, and thanked God for His faithfulness.

When it comes to money, there could be no more profound truth than what that precious dentist stated: "It's not mine; it's God's money." Those simple words are *the one crucial truth you need to know about money.*

WHAT'S IN YOUR WALLET?

For most people, when they think about legacy, the first thing that usually comes to mind is the money aspect. In Webster's dictionary, the initial definition for *legacy* is "money or property bequeathed by a will."

The wealthy and famous have always been interested in legacy. They know that they will have accumulated wealth to leave and understand their responsibility to manage those assets properly. Those who accomplish something noteworthy know they are assured of a place in history upon which their heirs can build.

Here is the truth: we will all leave a legacy *by design or default*. Will yours be successful or fledgling?

I want to help you design an *intentional, successful* legacy.

Jim Elliott said, "He is no fool who gives what he cannot keep to gain what he cannot lose."[2] Martin Luther, the German theologian and reformer, said, "I have held many things in my hands, and I have lost them all. But whatever I have placed in God's hands, that I still possess."

It is not an overstatement to say that everything about our lives and the legacy we intend to leave hinges on how we handle our money. Our handling of money, or its handling of us, determines whether or not the door of finances becomes an exit or entrance to a successful legacy.

It begins by having a proper perspective of money. Is money just a necessary evil? Do you find yourself always wanting more material things than you have the money to buy? How do you handle the seasons of lack or loss, or those times when you are lavishing in blessings?

Is money a blessing or a curse?

It's up to you!

Money has an inherent power. What we choose to do with the power of money determines whether it blesses or curses our lives and the lives of those around and beyond us.

The Bible is straightforward on this subject. It contains 2,350 verses on the subject of money, twice as many as on faith and prayer, and more than on heaven and hell combined. It's clear that money is an important indicator of our values. Equally as important is to understand how our money directly impacts our children and their legacy for generations.

The Heart of the Matter

Money is a very accurate measure of a man's values. The true measure of a person's belief is not their *feelings* but their *dealings*—specifically with money. "For where your treasure is, there your heart will be also" (Matt. 6:21).

Your dealing with money is a clear indicator of who you are and what are the real "heart-to-heart" issues of your life. What is at the core of your heart will either stifle or stimulate your legacy.

> **A checkbook is a theological document; it will tell you who and what you worship.**
>
> **—Billy Graham**

A dear friend of mine had a heart attack a few years ago. He must monitor the condition of his heart at all times. Any sign of a potential problem could be a matter of life or death. Your heart should be constantly monitored as well, and you can check on its condition by asking these questions:

- Where are my treasures?

- What do I value?

- What are my priorities?

- How is this expressed with my finances?

- Is there alignment between the two, or are they in conflict?

Open Heart, Open Heaven

An accumulation of blessings is one of the laws that govern God's kingdom. Why? His blessings are so abundant that we cannot receive all of them in this life. (See Malachi 3:10–13; Luke 6:38.)

We have an eternal bank account, and every day we make deposits and withdrawals. These deposits are a sure thing with a high rate of return. No investment could pay greater returns than the deliberate efforts of a generational-driven lifestyle.

We sometimes miss the wonder of God's favor by failing to see His generational view of blessings. We can be so shortsighted. We can fail to anticipate how an act of faithfulness on our part can lead to an act of favor on God's part generations down the line. Your grandchildren are credited with your acts of obedience. Don't limit God's blessings to just you and just the here and now.

God will bless your giving for generations to come. The great-grandchild that was in the seed of Abraham received the blessings of tithing nearly one hundred years before he entered into the world. Your giving is linked to generations. This revelation about how God viewed Abraham's tithe may be the most defining theological principle of this book. God gave credit of one generation's obedience to three generations down the line. What an awesome responsibility. I am directly determining blessings for my great-great-grandchildren. "Even Levi [the priests], who receives tithes, paid tithes through Abraham, so to speak, for he was still in the loins of his father" (Heb. 7:9–10).

Don't miss this truth.

When you and I act in obedience in our giving, we do not act alone. Generations are giving through us. It takes more than one generation to receive the "pressed-down, shaken-together, and running-over" blessings of giving (Luke 6:38). Because of this teaching, I can say that through my biological forefathers—through the obedience of my parents and their parents—I have been giving of my tithe for over one hundred years, although I am only fifty.

I live a life that exceeds what could be produced in one generation of giving. I have lived in houses I did not build and eaten of vineyards I did not plant. I am benefiting from God's faithfulness, which cannot be created or contained in one generation.

Likewise, when we hold back, we are setting a genetic pattern that will leave its influence for future generations. The ploy of the enemy is to distract each of us from establishing a lifestyle of giving for our lineage. It isn't hard to distract us in the area of giving. We get our focus diverted by plasma TVs, clothing sales, new technology, and golf clubs that will improve our game. After all, how can we be expected to thrive when we don't have a Rolex watch or a Louis Vuitton purse?

What acquisition could possibly be more important than the blessing you give your children and grandchildren by being a covenant giver? What object, what *must-have* purchase that you cannot pass by is worth shutting the windows of heaven off from your legacy?

> **We buy things we don't need with money we don't have to impress people we don't like.**

We cannot allow temporal circumstances to interrupt our investment in our legacy. When sincere Christians neglect or negate the responsibility of establishing or expanding the financial legacy of the kingdom, the enemy wins, and our children lose. "Seek first the kingdom of God and His righteousness, and all these things shall be added to you" (Matt. 6:33).

THE GOOD LIFE

Some Christians forget that one day we will rule and reign with Christ—right here on Earth. Have you ever thought about how we will live? Will Christians live in the big houses? Will we enjoy the wealth of the world's riches? If it will be right then, what makes it wrong now?

Prosperity is not a sin. It is the result of godly legacies that have been blessed by the favor of God. We read in the Scriptures of Jesus telling His disciples that God wanted them to enjoy good things. In Luke 12:32, we read, "It is your Father's good pleasure to give you the kingdom."

The apostle Paul reminded us of God's view on creation when he wrote, "For every creature of God is good, and *nothing is to be refused* if it is received with thanksgiving" (1 Tim. 4:4). He also stated, "Command those who are rich in this present age not to be haughty, nor to trust in uncertain riches but in the living God, *who gives us richly all things to enjoy*" (2 Tim. 6:17, emphasis added).

King David described what would follow those who dwell in God's house: "Surely goodness and mercy shall follow me all the days of my life; and I will dwell in the house of the LORD forever." (Ps. 23:6).

And James, the first bishop of the church, says it best: "Every good gift and every perfect gift is from above, and comes down from the Father of lights, with whom there is no variation or shadow of turning" (James 1:17).

God wants us to enjoy and live the good life. The good life is the *God* life! Our lives bring glory to God when—through the principles of God's Word—we live the abundant life that His Word promises.

Prosperity is not a disease that we should be trying to avoid. Prosperity is a healthy sign that you are living in and by kingdom rules. Yet prosperity will test our hearts.

In his book *Money, Possessions and Eternity*, Randy Alcorn tells the story of a persecuted Romanian pastor who told a group of ministers: "In my experience, 95 percent of the believers who face the test of persecution pass it, while 95 percent who face the test of prosperity fail it."[3]

The *test* of prosperity?

John Steinbeck once wrote to Adlai Stevenson, "A strange species we are. We can stand anything God and nature throws at us, save plenty. If I wanted to destroy a nation, I would give it too much, and I would have it on its knees, miserable, greedy and sick."[4]

For many, prosperity seems to stir more division than delight. It may be because we aren't thinking the same thoughts and concepts when we say prosperity. Here are some nonnegotiables regarding prosperity.

THE PRINCIPLES OF PROSPERITY

Contentment

The Scriptures teach us that contentment is the first step toward a prosperity that is pure and productive. The greatest gain you will have in your portfolio will be contentment. No matter what state of affairs you find yourself in, you can be—you must be—content. You will be amazed at what kind of legacy you can build when your appetite for things is in check. Contentment will guide you to developing true eternal values that not only will be rewarded in heaven but will also have great benefits to those who inherit your legacy here on Earth.

> Now godliness with contentment is great gain. For we brought nothing into this world, and it is certain we can carry nothing out. And having food and clothing, with these we shall be

content....For the love of money is a root of all kinds of evil, for which some have strayed from the faith in their greediness, and pierced themselves through with many sorrows.

—1 Timothy 6:6–8, 10

Constraint

What you can't control, controls you. The discipline you demonstrate with your finances will determine the blessing that God can entrust to you. When I get into my car, I start the car with my foot on the brakes. I want to know before I accelerate with any power that I can stop the car if I need to. So it is with money. Before you accelerate your power to make money, learn how to put the brakes on your spending.

Contentment is best understood by thinking about the possibility of losing everything that you own— and then getting it back!

Poverty in the Western world is often the result of a lack of restraint and not a lack of resources. If your appetite and ambition for possessions are in check, you will be achieving the "blessed to be a blessing" life God has for you.

A balanced perspective on prosperity could very well start by balancing your checkbook. Having a *budget* prepares you for the *bountiful* blessings God wants you to have.

Change

You can't do the same things over and over and expect different results; that's insanity. Wealth will come based on your willingness to change. I'm not talking about pocket change. I'm talking about getting to the core changes that may need to take place before you can experience true prosperity.

Ask yourself these questions:

- How do I feel about wealth?

- What kind of attitude do I have toward wealthy people?

- When I see magnificent homes, art, or jewelry, how do I respond? With jealousy? Judgment?

Monitor your heart; if you have any issues you have not faced, take a good look at your heart—because that's where everything starts.

Pay attention to your heart, or you will pay the consequences. Remember, you don't get in life what you want; you get what you are, and you are the secret "issues" of your heart. If you are prone to attack the wealthy, you most likely will not attract the wealth. Don't let your unresolved issues go to your children's *tissues*.

"All the gold and silver is mine," says the Lord. (See Haggai 2:8.) If that is true, then it should be looked upon as a blessing. Begin by respecting and responding to the blessings others are receiving. If you can rejoice in someone else's blessings, then you are qualifying yourself for the same.

The pathway to prosperity begins as Jesus taught: first, with the way you handle other people's money; then with the little you are given; then the much that God will give you (Luke 19:17).

Character

Only a pure vessel can carry the blessings. Character counts when it comes to wealth—not just in what you may gain but also in what you give, and not just what you give but why you give.

It's been said that life comes down to three things—learn, earn, and then return. We live the first part of our life learning. We then must earn our living. The greatest season is when we find worthy causes to return what we've learned and earned back to society. This includes legal instruments of wills and trusts that can continue giving through our children and/or church long after we're gone.

There is much that has been written both on how to obtain wealth and how to distribute that wealth. Live by the biblical standards of finances, and you will see great fruit that will manifest in your legacy. Principles will attract principals. Following the wisdom of God is not only right—it will make right things happen to and through you.

Prosperity is part of the power that we must step up to. Influence and affluence are our right and responsibility. If we are naïve or slothful of this role in kingdom living, we will either misuse prosperity or allow it to be used by others who are neither sincere nor responsible.

Giving is the biblical synonym for prosperity. God places no gap between the getting and giving of wealth. It's assumed that you must have much to give much. So the gift of giving "with liberality" in Romans 12:8 is another way of acknowledging the gift of making money. It's a gift. Do you have it?

Do you see seed, or do you see need?

Truth is, your money is a crucial key for your legacy.

You don't have to be a wealthy tycoon to have the leverage for a meaningful financial legacy. It begins with an understanding of the dynamics of giving. Let's learn the four-step process to spiritual maturity and legacy building through our finances.

Four Stages of Giving

Legacy is setting a generational strategy with your resources and relationships. There are four stages of how we live our lives in relation to money.

Live to live: *survival*

We all begin life as takers. We live to live. That's all we do. Beginning with the fight upstream as one of four hundred million sperm making its way to the egg in our mother's womb, it is a fight for survival. We start out plugged to the cord of someone else's lifeline.

We enter into the world totally dependent on other people. It may be our mother, father, or a caregiver, but someone better see to it that our every need is met. It doesn't take long, even as a baby, to realize that you are in control. It registers in your mind that when you cry, someone is going to come to your aid. "It's all about me" is the mandatory theme song of early life. We take, take, and take some more.

Stand outside of yourself and make note of the way you live. Are you a taker? Are you in survival mode? What would those who work with you say about you? Those at your church? Your family? Do you leave more than you take? It's time to get unplugged and start a lifestyle of giving.

Give to live: *share*

Giving to live is part of the development of becoming interdependent. You recognize that if you are going to get what you want in life, you will have to give a little. You develop a "give-and-take" way of living and learn to negotiate with those around you.

As a child we learned this as we played with other children. We learned that by giving a little (even if the motives are not pure) we could receive, *if* we are willing to give a little bit of ourselves.

This kind of giving is often little more than a form of manipulation and not true giving. It is not giving in its purest form. The motives of our hearts become obvious when others do not respond to our giving in the manner we think they should, and we become hurt and angry. Our giving still has strings attached. It may not be that thick "cord" we had as a baby, but we expect to get something back from our giving—even if it is just ego gratification.

> **Man is born with his fist clenched but dies with his hands wide open.**
>
> **—The Talmud**

This can go on for a prolonged period of time. Some people stay at this stage of life until the very end. When that happens, the full expansion of the nature of giving is stopped and legacy is threatened.

Give to give: *sow*

Every heartbeat provides an opportunity for motive and movement to merge into a moment of pure giving. The first time you follow this pure motive is the turning point of your life. In that very moment, you find the meaning of life—giving.

The flow of giving goes against every instinct of our carnal natures. Our selfish motives are reinforced by logic: look out for yourself, take before you are taken from, and hoard for a rainy day.

The best word to describe giving is *sowing*. The world is a field, and your deeds are seeds. Sowing and reaping, reaping and sowing—that is the circle of life. You are now in that circle. As you have opened your heart and hands to give, life will open up to you.

Within the very reaping of your giving is more seed for sowing. You cannot give yourself out of love, forgiveness, caring, or sharing. The more you give, the more you receive. The only way to stop the receiving is to stop the giving. It would be hard to imagine the possibility that you could be blessed even greater—but wait, there's more!

Live to give: *significance*

Having stumbled onto the joy that comes from giving, you develop a discerning gift of giving. Sowing is good, but sowing with strategy is better. Helping people in need is good, but solving problems that keep people from being in need is better. Like the old saying goes, "Give a man a fish, and you feed him for a day. Give him a fishing pole, and you feed him for a lifetime." Legacy giving goes one step further; it says, "Buy the pond!" With proper strategy, we can use our assets and our accumulated wealth to be giving into wealth-producing projects long after our life on this side of eternity is over.

When you allow the principles of prosperity to rule in your heart, you will enjoy the blessings. Your children will inherit not just the wealth but also the virtues you have practiced.

> Command those who are rich in this present age not to be haughty, nor to trust in uncertain riches but in the living God, who gives us richly all things to enjoy. Let them do good, that they be rich in good works, ready to give, willing to share, storing up for themselves a good foundation for the time to come, that they may lay hold of eternal life.
>
> —1 Timothy 6:17–19

THE LEGACY REVOLUTION

Bill Gates has decided to leave the day-to-day operations of Microsoft in order to devote all of his time to the foundation that he and his wife, Melinda, founded and funded.[5] The foundation has $31 billion in assets. Within days of the announcement, another of the world's wealthiest entrepreneurs made an equally shocking statement. William Buffet will give $37 billion to the Gates's foundation. He insists that the money be spent during the lifetime of Bill and Melinda Gates.[6]

In 2005, Boston College's Center on Wealth and Philanthropy conducted a survey of ninety-one people with assets above $30 million. Sixty-five percent said they planned to donate more of their wealth during their lifetimes than in their estates. Sanford Weill, former CEO of Citigroup, who has given away $600 million in the past fifteen years, says, "People realize you can't take it with you."[7]

It's a lot better to do a lot of this philanthropy while you're still alive and have the energy. We can use our brainpower to make the world a better place now—not to leave a bunch of money that will be around in a hundred years.

Many financial advisors believe that the "giving while living" philanthropic plan will become a model for how to achieve maximum impact and witness the results of your giving in your lifetime. Many parents also involve their children in their charitable plans, using philanthropy.

Is this the beginning of a revolution? Why wait until you die to distribute your wealth? Who says a legacy begins when our lives end?

This is the revolution: live your legacy now!

FINANCES CARRY OUR LEGACY

The accumulation of wealth for wealth alone can become destructive to you and your children. Prosperity growth without purpose will destroy either you or your legacy—maybe both.

Growth for growth's sake, without regard to the intent, is the goal of cancer. Cancer will grow until it destroys the very body it lives in.

Why is it crucial to connect our finances to our legacy? Our giving has generational consequences. The blessing and/or cursing determined by our pattern of giving will have more impact on the generation following us than most of us understand. This single issue alone may be a stumbling block to our own children and certainly is "infecting" our nation.

> **He who gives while he lives gets to know where it goes.**
>
> **—Percy Ross**

We all understand the dynamics of accumulation, whether the accumulation is debt or savings. Compound interest can work for or against you.

In the United States it has become acceptable to carry a large amount of debt. Often this debt results from financing a self-serving, short-term, superficial lifestyle with credit card spending. After you add on the interest, servicing the debt becomes a never-ending burden.

If you do not have the liberty to give because of an already extended budget from excessive consumption, your life is based on faulty values. When your resources don't incorporate giving, you transfer those faulty values to the next generation.

The Scriptures teach the law of "firstfruits." (See Leviticus 23:9–21; Proverbs 3:9–10.) The first of everything is to be given to the Lord. It is a law that helps keep our priorities straight.

In the Old Testament, this was strictly enforced, as is illustrated by the example of the firstfruit of the animals that were to be offered as a sacrifice unto the Lord. If the firstborn of an animal was usable for the temple (sacrifice or other use of service), then it could be received. If not, you would need to sell the animal—like a firstborn donkey—and give the "redemptive" value to the Lord's work. If you could not sell the animal, then you were to break the neck of the donkey. If it was not going to be used by the Lord, it was not going to be used by anyone else![8] (See Exodus 13:13; 34:19–20, 26; Leviticus 27:26–28.)

> When first things are put first, second things are not suppressed but increased.
> —C. S. Lewis

This sounds drastic. But God was training the people that if the law of giving firstfruits was violated, the consequences would be worse than a dead donkey. Today, as a result of people drifting from the "first-things-first" principle, we have growing debt that is breaking the neck of marriages, churches, and our country. The enemy and the system of greed and indulgence have every intention of getting to your money and the positive potential it has as seed for the next generation. Until you and I accept the nonnegotiable laws of giving, we will continue to be broken by the consequences. You can violate a law of God, but you cannot break it.

The great universities, hospitals, and mission organizations of the Western world were established by Christian leaders who were not afraid to give up momentary pleasures for long-term purposes. This foundation of giving is one of our legacies as a nation. What will this generation do with that legacy?

We are facing a serious challenge at getting subsequent generations to adopt the *faith of our fathers* into their belief system. A nation like America can lose a generation of givers with one baton drop. The good news is that giving is making a comeback as a way of living for this generation. The Bible warns us not to say to ourselves, "'My power and the might of my hand have gained me this wealth.' And you shall remember the LORD your God, for it is He who gives you power to get wealth, *that He may establish His covenant which He swore to your fathers*, as it is this day" (Deut. 8:17–18, emphasis added).

With a legacy, you establish a generational strategy for your resources and relationships. A legacy linked to finances becomes a powerful instrument.

SCARED TO LIFE

Stephen King tells of his personal epiphany regarding his perspective of money:

> A couple of years ago, I found out what "you can't take it with you" means. I found out while I was lying in a ditch at the side of a country road, covered with mud and blood and with the tibia of my right leg poking out the side of my jeans like a branch of a tree taken down in a thunderstorm. I had a MasterCard in my wallet, but when you're lying in a ditch with broken glass in your hair, no one accepts MasterCard....
>
> We come in naked and broke. We may be dressed when we go out, but we're just as broke....All the money you will earn...all the stocks you will buy, all the mutual funds and precious metals you will trade—all of that is mostly smoke and mirrors....It's still going to be a quarter-past getting late whether you tell the time on a Timex or a Rolex....
>
> I want you to consider making your lives one long gift to others, and why not? All you have is on loan anyway....It's [the world] not a pretty picture, but we have the power to help, the power to

change. And why should we refuse? Because we're going to take it with us?...

I ask you to begin the next great phase of your life by giving, and to continue as you begin. I think you'll find in the end that you got far more than you ever had, and did more good than you ever dreamed.[9]

This man has used his gift to scare millions with his fictional stories. This time he speaks a pure truth that should frighten us if we fail to take heed.

Do you believe that eternity matters? Do you believe that how you live and give will have an impact on those who will follow you?

Giving, like prayer, never dies. It is not a one-time action. It lives forever in the eternal realm. (See Acts 10; Revelation 5:8; 8:5.)

Legacy is more than just a will that you get a lawyer to set up for you. It literally takes a *will*—as in will power! That is why you must buy into the truth that everything matters. Life is not just personal but generational with eternal consequences!

There will be times when doing right or going that extra mile is not going to be easy. Your commitment to a generational-eternal-driven life must be embedded within you. Money is a quick and easy way to measure where you are from both of those perspectives.

Our real worth is what will be ours in eternity.

God Is a Gardener: Sowing and Reaping

God has put a seed in your hand.

The metaphor of *seed* contains the model of God's way of bringing truth to mankind. From the beginning we are made aware of the law of sowing and reaping: "And the Lord God planted a garden..." (Gen. 2:8).

God is a gardener? "While the earth remains, seedtime and harvest...shall not cease" (Gen. 8:22).

The truth that God has brought forth to us could be spoken in one word—*seed*! The idea that everything comes from a seed is found from Genesis to Revelation. The Bible begins in the garden and ends in the garden. The *seedtime and harvest* concept is so imbedded in the Scriptures that Jesus Himself said the kingdom of God is a "seed."

What is the kingdom of God like?...like a mustard seed, which a man took and put in his garden; and it grew and became a large tree, and the birds of the air nested in its branches.

—LUKE 13:18–19

Legacy is in a seed! The potential of every seed is beyond calculation. The tree that bears your seed will be the start of a legacy that you cannot even comprehend at this point.

Your deliberate actions, though seemingly small, are big when God is in them. A great legacy is in your hand.

YOUR FINANCES AS SEED

Money is seed.

Once Jeannie and I were having lunch with Dr. Schuller in his office overlooking the Crystal Cathedral. He shared a principle that has had enormous impact on how we think about money. Dr. Schuller said:

I took a lot of criticism over the cost of the Crystal Cathedral. It was over twenty million dollars, and many thought it was a waste. But the actual cost of the raw material for the building was a few million dollars; the rest went to truck drivers, glasscutters, and construction workers. The money paid mortgage payments, car payments, and college tuition. It helped fulfill the dreams of many people.[10]

That concept formed a new paradigm in my mind. My money is seed. So what if I pay a few extra dollars for a car. The money is not going to the actual car; it's going to people. I'm not wasting money; I'm investing it in the lives of people.

If we could see our money as seed, we would link to a more meaningful purpose for the financial means that we have.

SEEDING INTO THE NEXT GENERATION

What seeds of giving will the next generation inherit from you?

Jeannie has a passion for the people of Uganda. On a recent missions trip along with our missionary friend Evelyn Komuntale, she was able to meet the Pygmy people in Uganda. These precious people are becoming the *breakout* generation from past generations of primitive living.

Not far removed from what men would live like five hundred years ago, they are seeking a new and better life for their children. Jeannie has taken music recorders (flutes) for them. The joy and the appreciation of the people are overwhelming. It's been like stepping back in time to reach out and bring them into the twenty-first century. Evelyn's organization, Outreach to Africa, has been working to improve their nutritional eating by helping them plant gardens.[11]

However, Evelyn and others can't just give these precious people the seed. They would eat it. She has had to talk with them first and explain the concept of sowing the seed to reap more in the future.

That's a critical lesson to learn not only in farming but also in our own lives. You have to make a choice. Is this opportunity for me? Is it for now?

Legacy is taking the long-term view of life. It's remarkable how a little seed, a little decision, can have a huge impact when you leave it committed to the future.

Will you eat your seed with fear, or will you plant your seed with faith?

The giving lifestyle will bring you into a world that not only will bless you but also will put your seed in a position of harvest.

WHERE THERE IS NO WILL, THERE IS NO WAY

Legacy is not just about what you have become, nor is it just about what you leave and whom you leave it to. It's about facing God and telling Him what you have done with what He entrusted to you.

How tragic it would be to leave this earth with assets that you had gained, only to face God with them having been lost—carelessly—because you lacked the foresight to establish a proper legacy.

Be certain that your legacy will be protected and projected for generations to come. Every seed sown will matter—every harvest will have eternal rewards and responsibilities.

PART FOUR

Your Future

The good you do today is the gift you give to your lineage tomorrow. The equity you infuse into your legacy is limited only by your imaGENEation! The dream you dream today becomes your future legacy.

CHAPTER 11

Look Back to See Forward
Are you wearing your designer genes?

Written down so we'll know how to live well and right, to understand what life means and where it's going; a manual for living, for learning what's right and just and fair; to teach the inexperienced the ropes and give our young people a grasp on reality. There's something here also for seasoned men and women, still a thing or two for the experienced to learn—fresh wisdom to probe and penetrate, the rhymes and reasons of wise men and women.
—PROVERBS 1:1–16, THE MESSAGE

THINK ABOUT THIS. WE MAKE THE MOST IMPORTANT DECISIONS IN our lives at a time when we are the least qualified to make them. By the time we have gained wisdom and insight, it often feels like it has come too little, too late, and with too many mistakes.

But legacy comes and takes us by the hand and leads us down a well-worn path paved with the experiences of our forefathers. We embrace the strength of the "great cloud of witnesses" that eagerly celebrates the running of our laps toward our destiny. We began our race where theirs ended. They have a vested interest in the outcome of this human race that we are in.

There are dreams that were left on the track. Some were too far out of reach. Some of their dreams were rudely interrupted by circumstances beyond their control. They are running vicariously through you.

163

Feel their strength, hear their whispers of support, and draw from their experiences as you make critical decisions in the race you are running. Their blood cells are running through your veins and ringing in your heart. Heed the call.

God uses an accumulation of the principle of "deeds to seeds" to impact and influence the generations. There is an accrual that has been gathering in the account of your lineage. You will have your turn to contribute. First, you must come to learn the power of equity. Equity is the positive side of why everything about us matters.

Much has been written about the iniquity of our past. Many psychologists and even some pastors counsel us as if our past determines our future. Even in this book I have shown you through Scripture, science, and studies of social behavior that in every deed there is a seed!

Besides presenting a sobering responsibility, an awareness of the importance of the seeds planted by our forefathers raises some questions that must be answered:

- Is my DNA responsible for my failures?

- Am I limited to the life that my parents lived before me?

- What if I decide to live and express my life with different values?

A major automobile company bought a smaller company of a popular sports car many years ago. Though the car was admired, the servicing of the car was horrendous. The new company cleverly developed an ad campaign that said, "We've kept all the good things, and the rest is history!"

That is what Christ did for us—He has left the good, and the rest is HIStory!

At the moment of conversion, you received a *new you* in Christ. It's wonderful to know you have a fresh start, but what of all the good from your past? Does that just go away? What of the character and charisma that is in your lineage, and the sacrifice and successful efforts that your forefathers gave in their lifetimes? Did their good deeds go with them to the grave? Thankfully no!

The promise of your future is contained in the equity of your blood-line. I know it sounds too good to be true, but all the bad stuff that happened to and through you was wiped clean at the cross. You have a clean slate. It's a clean slate, but not a clear slate. This is an important distinction—you have a redeemed history, but it's not a removed history. The bad has been cleaned, but the good remains. You get to have your legacy (the cake) and live (eat) it, too.

Everything you do in your lifetime adds to an accumulation of deeds in your generational stock. God is a legacy builder, and legacy takes time to build.

Each generation builds on the knowledge and experiences of those who have gone before them. We would not survive if we lost all science, history, and educational advancements with each generation. If every generation had to start over, we would lose the quality of life as we know it.

THE EQUITY IN YOUR BLOODLINE

One of my dearest friends, advisors, and mentors was a pastor by the name of Jim Roam. Jim loved to defy everyone's expectations, and he stayed ahead of the curve when it came to innovative and progressive approaches to ministry. So his friends, myself included, were surprised when he decided at around the age of forty to give up his thriving church in Ohio to move back to St. Louis and help his ailing father.

Jim served his father's church for eight years. His time there was often frustrating and difficult for him. He and his wife, Sharon, had moved there more out of a sense of family obligation than true personal conviction. Finally, he moved on and developed a thriving ministry in Phoenix before passing away a few years ago.

Over the years, I've often wondered about the meaning of his move to St. Louis. Was it a mistake? Was it a bad decision? Or was there some sense of destiny in his choice to honor his father?

The answer came to me during a recent conversation I had with Jim's son, Brent. Brent told me of an experience he had enjoyed a few weeks earlier. He said he was interviewing for a job in one of the partner's offices on the thirty-sixth floor of the biggest law firm in Missouri. As he was answering the questions put to him by the partner in the firm, he looked out the window and saw the train yard where his great-grandfather had worked decades before he was even born. He saw the bus station where his grandfather had labored as a bus mechanic fifty years earlier.

He realized that his father, Jim, had been born and grew up in a neighborhood not far from the firm. He took in the brilliance of the St. Louis arch and the majesty of the Mississippi River, which flowed just a few hundred yards away. And he knew this was where he belonged. Two weeks later, Brent was offered the position of a summer associate at the firm. Jim's time in St. Louis was not a mistake—it was a necessary step in the fulfillment of his legacy.

Understanding the equity in your bloodline is a great place to start. So much good is waiting for you when you take stock of your personal heritage and history. The answers to many questions can be found when you explore your lineage.

> **Like riding on a donkey backwards, we live life forward, but only understand it backwards.**
>
> **—Old Chinese Proverb**

Inventory of your DNA will show the accumulative attitudes and actions of your ancestors. The character and charisma that is in your lineage does not just go away. It is placed in your stock and is accessible for you and for generations to come.

In this hallowed stockroom are shelves upon shelves of resources available to you. You are contributing to those same stockroom shelves every single day. Those who follow in your lineage will have even more resources to draw upon, depending on what you added to the shelves in your lifetime.

You will see the hand of God at work as far back as you can research.

This understanding of your past could revolutionize your future more than finding a bank account with millions of dollars in your name.

You are going to be amazed by the valuable information you will find in your family's past. Questions will be answered, instincts will be confirmed, and new talents will be released with confidence. You will know what is your heritage, and that will help you discover what is your legacy.

Equity is recognizing the good in your past and investing it into your future. I want you to see your equity as potential material for the betterment of mankind. See the actions, adventures, tests, and trials as precious material at your disposal for making the world a better place. Think of the ways you can use your legacy to have lasting value.

Christ, our Mediator, has put our negative past under lock and key and has actually thrown the key away. All the good that we do is placed in our future *stock* and is accessible for generations to come.

Use a sanctified (selective) memory to explore the equity that is in your lineage. An inventory of your DNA will show the accumulative attitudes and actions of your ancestors. You may discover the courage necessary to make your next move in the pages of your family history.

What if drawing on your past opens the door to a pain too horrific to allow access? As I reflect on what you might be facing, I walk softly toward your heart. You may have memories of an alcoholic parent, abuse by a close family member, or a painful divorce—possibly all three.

At a men's retreat that I conducted several years ago, sobering and stunning confessions of the men opened a floodgate of painful mistakes and past misery. Men were sobbing with humble, brutal honesty about their tormenting secrets. A man we'll call Ted stood up and, shaking uncontrollably, shared the horrific abuse he suffered at the hands of his father. Seeing what damage this had upon him and his siblings, it led him to have a vasectomy so as to ensure that he would not ever be capable of repeating the same hurt to another generation. We wept in shock and sadness. This did not need to happen. There is a healing that can resolve the hurt. You do not have to be imprisoned by the iniquity of your lineage. God can convert the iniquity into equity. It all starts in your heart. One act on your part will change everything.

There is so much valuable history in your lineage; don't sacrifice it for one event or person. I will show you a path that will take you to a greater purpose. Will you take it?

The path is forgiveness.

Forgive!

We have all heard the one-liners about forgiveness. At some point we need to find and own one. Here is the one that did it for me:

"Not forgiving someone is like drinking poison and expecting the other person to die!"

Besides, you have been given a fresh start from God that included a lot of forgiveness yourself! There is only one joy greater than being forgiven; it is when we choose to forgive others.

Escape from the road of destruction. Turn around. The destination for an unforgiving heart ends the same for everyone, no matter where your starting point is or what started you on the path. The end will be pain and time lost painfully in your legacy. Forgiveness is always the fast track to a new route to your destiny.

> And whenever you stand praying, if you have anything against anyone, forgive him, that your Father in heaven may also forgive you your trespasses.
>
> —MARK 11:25

You may ask, who pays the bill for the offense? Good question.

Jesus Christ paid the bill.

A story I heard years ago illustrates this point. The judge, who was up for reelection, had a brother who violated an ordinance. A lenient sentence would seem unjust; a harsh sentence would seem unfair. The verdict was scheduled just one day before the election.

The courtroom was filled with reporters waiting for the verdict. Whispers hummed through the crowd like bees. The judge spoke: "On this day I declare the man before me guilty of the violation. As a result he will be ordered to pay the full fine of ten thousand dollars!"

The judge then took off his robe, took ten thousand dollars from his wallet, and paid the fine himself.

Justice and mercy were upheld that day. So was the judge's job.

God demands justice. Sin must be judged. Many say that God would not punish anyone if He were a God of love. He is also a God of justice. The Adolf Hitlers of our world cannot commit hideous acts of violence against millions of people and die with no recompense. What kind of God would look the other way and ignore that?

God stepped down from His throne and wrapped Himself in flesh. He became a man to pay the price of sin on the cross of Calvary— justice and mercy, hand in hand.

Forgiveness is not the condoning of a wrong done. It's the confidence that God will judge the unrighteous deed. Only God could do both. We can do neither.

Our part is to be instruments of forgiveness. Do the right thing. In that single act, you sign a check that releases the funds of equity you will need to build your legacy.

The Secret of Success Is Your Secrets

Just how potent are your secrets? Is it possible to separate our private thoughts and attitudes from our public traits and actions? Not according to the Scriptures. Jesus taught us that what we think in secret would be shouted from the housetop. (See Matthew 6:1–6.)

This is not saying that God is a tattletale. The truth of this verse is not a threat but a fact. Secrets will be revealed now or later—in us or in our descendants. At first, having one's thoughts being shouted on the housetop—literally through my children and their children's children—may seem intimidating. But in truth, it is an incredible secret to success to discover that you can *think* your way to another level of living.

Allow me to illustrate.

I am always coming out of or going into a diet.

Is it genetics? We won't go there.

I do well when I make myself accountable. Jeannie and I were once on a diet that required us to write down everything we ate. Of course, we would weigh ourselves every day. I was doing all right until I had a speaking engagement for three nights that took me past an In-N-Out Burger restaurant. (If you don't know about this particular food chain, you will fall short of relating to the temptation I was facing.) The first night was tempting, but I resisted. I wavered the second night, but by the third night I had given in. Disguising my voice, I ordered a double cheeseburger, fries, and, of course, a diet coke.

Afterward, I needed to hide the evidence. When I pulled into the driveway, I cleverly tucked the bag deep into the garbage container so Jeannie would not see or smell the incriminating evidence. With a breath mint in my mouth and a smirk on my face, I climbed into bed. It was going to be awkward trying to explain the added weight on the scale the next morning, but that turned out to be unnecessary. As God would have it, Jeannie had thrown the wrong portion of a bill away and had to go deep into the trash to retrieve it. Wouldn't you know she discovered the evidence?

There went my little secret.

Whom was I fooling? Just because no one saw me eating in the night did not mean it would not be revealed in the light.

My secrets ultimately become my success or my regrets. As I said earlier, you don't get in life what you want—you get what you are— and you are what you think. You are your secrets.

That's not a bad thing. Turn it around and see the good God meant that truth to be for our benefit. If you become positive and pure in your intentions, you start a secret conspiracy of good things for you and your lineage.

From your heart you will bring forth treasures that enrich your legacy. The way you react to gossip, the attitude you have toward authority, the effort you put forth at work when no one is paying attention, these will become the secrets that will one day be shouted from the rooftop of your legacy.

Secrets of our conscience and character shape our personal, generational, and eternal destiny. Think a good thought now. Now imagine it as a seed. Guard it and nurture it. One day that secret seed will bloom into a successful deed for all to see.

STORY TIME: THE LINKS TO YOUR LINEAGE

Another great way to tap the inventory of equity is to become a storyteller. Telling the stories of our past is a lost art. The absence of those priceless experiences keep us from taking advantage of our rich legacy. To tell the story of your legacy you need not only to write down and relive your stories, but you also need to research and dig out the stories to be found in your own family lineage.

Technology, movies and such, has taken the place of good ol' storytelling. The problem with Hollywood is that it doesn't know *our* stories. While you enjoy being entertained with the real and fictional stories of Hollywood, you are leaving unheard the dramatic and daring adventures of your own life. Buried in your genetic bunkers are treasured tales from and for your destiny just waiting to be told.

Tucked away in your own family stories you may find the answers to the questions you have about why you do what you do. The deep resonating stirrings that are sparked by certain events that take place in your life will find meaning and substance by searching out the *stockroom* of your own family legacy. By looking within your family legacy inventory you will be able to fill the gaps and voids in your heart as you search for the directions to your destiny.

Why are you drawn to certain causes? Why do you desire to do things that seem so unusual? Where do some of those crazy ideas you often have come from?

I love to probe and uncover my equity with my parents (Jeannie's and mine). The stories they tell reveal so much. When I hear about how my father-in-law started his business with five dollars and a rented trailer, I can understand why Jeannie is unafraid to go after big things with so little in her hand. Her father, Odie, took discarded materials and sold them until he accumulated the means to begin a business that became one of the top lumber stores of his day.

At the age of fifty, Jeannie went after her airplane pilot's license, responding to the legacy gene from her father, who was an airplane simulator instructor pilot during World War II. That instinct was in her inventory just waiting to be tapped.

Why do I love missions? Why would I go to Venezuela and fall in love with the wonderful people of that nation? Why I said yes to John Maxwell's last minute call was beyond me. As I hung up the phone I thought to myself, "I must be crazy! That country is a political hotbed."

But as I stood in front of eighteen hundred pastors in Valencia, Venezuela, I remembered! Many years ago just after he had started his church in Indiana, my father spent four to six weeks each year doing missions work in South America. When I was only five years old, I was telling people that when I grew up I was going to buy a motorcycle and preach the gospel to South America! It took forty-five years for that nearly forgotten boyish dream to happen—but it did (except for the part about arriving on a motorcycle)!

Everything Happens *for* You, Not *to* You

Every experience, the joy and sorrow, victories and mistakes, all the things that God has made work for the good are at your disposal. They become deposits that work for the good of you and your lineage.

Don't delete the drama that you have gone through. Sure, there may be stories that would bring shame to your lineage, but let humility guide you as you recollect the experiences and events in your past. Humility is a virtue that attracts God's favor. Humility and humor come from the same root word. Tell those stories about yourself that allow you and others to laugh. One of our family's pastimes is remembering and reliving those hilarious stories.

Tell the stories of your tragedies to triumphs also. The destiny of your DNA is released by the memories of your life's stories. Don't be ashamed. Give your legacy a voice.

Grasp the power of stories. You will tap that power when you understand that the difficult things that have happened in your life did not happen *to* you—they happened *for* you and for your legacy. "All things work together *for* good..." (Rom. 8:28, emphasis added).

I believe the apostle Paul was saying, "I know that no matter what comes my way, all things happen *for* me, not *to* me!" When you understand this, this one paradigm shift can convert all your experiences into the *good* column in your ledger—all things can become a positive deposit, not a negative withdrawal. It's ironic how humorous our horrible experiences become from the vantage point of looking backward at them with a positive perspective—add a little humility, then a little humor, and you end up with a lot of honor.

Until this present generation, it was common for children to spend long hours with their grandparents or even to live with them at some point in their lives. Do these words sound familiar? "Grandpa, tell me a story."

Grandpa would usually spin a tale about something that happened in an earlier period of his life. From the story, the child would learn who his grandpa is, how he lived his life, what the family stock is all about, and family rituals that must be preserved.

There is an old African saying: "When an old person dies, it's as if a library burns down." Who are the elders of your legacy? Who's managing the library for your children? How will the story of your life be remembered and retold? Do you want to leave it to chance? How can you show your descendants that they are part of a continuum that began before they were born and will continue after they leave?

For those of you who are part of an ever-increasing number of grandparents who are raising their grandchildren, I know the circumstances may not be the way you want them to be. But you have a chance to have a direct line of influence to the next generation. God takes what the enemy has meant for evil and turns it to good. It's a second chance to correct the areas where parents may have fallen short in raising their own children.

The Bible reminds us: "Only take heed to yourself, and diligently keep yourself, lest you forget the things your eyes have seen, and lest they depart from your heart all the days of your life. And teach them to your children and your grandchildren" (Deut. 4:9).

Stories are the stones that build a legacy, one upon another. The stories build a "memory museum" where our children can explore the world from which they have come. Buried treasure? That's what is in the hearts of our parents and their parents! Are you deliberately and gently laying down a foundation of legacy stones for the next generation to view and value?

Every story carries a part of the genetic make-up that will allow the next generation to know just who they are and what they can become. Don't let your stories go to the grave with you. You can live on forever in the stories that you give to your children's children.

This is your chance to influence eternity with your life.

You Look Better in Your Future

If you are over the age of thirty, you probably think you looked better in the past. Remember your high school picture? No matter how bad you thought that picture was at the time, I bet you look back now and see a young and fresh face that you really miss.

I'm here to tell you that from God's perspective, you look better in your future!

You must believe that your future will be better than your past. This is true regardless of whether your past has been exciting and overflowing with achievement and adventure or difficult and weighed down with misfortune and failure.

Whatever your interpretation of your life thus far, it is time to dream of an awesome tomorrow. It is time to imaGENE your future.

> **Develop the persistence to "see things through" and the positive perception to "see through things" so that nothing stops your legacy.**

I've written this book for people who feel a twinge of envy when they see someone with a clear and lucid vision. If you are not satisfied to let day after day go by with no apparent rhyme or reason, it's for you.

Say, "I will not be distracted or detoured by the lame and mundane. I want a life of purpose and legacy. I want meaning in my work and in my relationships. I want to know that I am on a mission, and I want to know what that mission is. I want that mission to live beyond me!"

Now is the time to plant seeds, pull the weeds, and nurture the garden of what your legacy will look like for the generations that follow.

PICTURE PERFECT

You look better in your future because you know things now that you simply could not have known earlier. You look better in your future because your supply of faith, hope, and love have blossomed.

The picture is clearer now. You see beyond your nose and eyes and ears and hair. You see the real you, the you who looks more like the pictures you've seen of your forefathers and heirs than you realized earlier. Even the wrinkles on your face are a map of your journey.

I love my father. There are so many things that I admire about him—his boldness, his never-say-die mind-set. Quite frankly, he is his name, *Frank*. He speaks his mind, and he'll speak yours if necessary.

However, his looks are not the thing I admire most about him. My mother, on the other hand, is a beautiful woman who looks twenty years younger than she is. I would love to look like her, but alas, I do not.

I do my best to disguise the DNA of my father's looks. I have grown a goatee, and I nurse each and every hair on my head. No matter how hard I try, my father waits for me every morning and looks me in the eye when I look in the mirror. There is no denying, I am my father's child.

Now I can understand what the apostle John meant when he said, "Whoever has been born of God does not sin, for *His seed* remains in him; and he cannot sin, because he has been born of God" (1 John 3:9, emphasis added).

That's the power of DNA.

Every time I look into the mirror of God's Word, I am reminded that I have the DNA of my heavenly Father. Without any effort or reliance on my flesh, I look and act like my heavenly Father more every day. I have a legacy of blessings and benefits coming to and through me. I am my heavenly Father's child.

CHAPTER 12

From Here to Eternity

Eternalizing your problems and potential

Stay with what you heard from the beginning, the original message. Let it sink into your life. If what you heard from the beginning lives in you, you will live deeply in both Son and Father. This is exactly what Christ promised: eternal life, real life!

—1 JOHN 2:25, THE MESSAGE

"YOU ARE NOT AFFECTING ETERNITY!" WERE THE WORDS ORAL ROBERTS heard God say that would change his life forever!

Living close to Oral and Evelyn Roberts has afforded Jeannie and me the privilege of spending countless hours with these legends of the faith.

When Evelyn went to be with the Lord, my first thought when we heard of her death was that she had spent her life serving and preferring Oral's ministry. Now God was granting her the honor of "going home" first.

A friend of mine was telling his daughter about Oral Roberts coming to speak at their church a few years ago. "That's not possible!" she exclaimed. "Oral Roberts is not a person—it's a university." That's the power of a legacy. Say what you will about Oral, his impact on our world is beyond questioning.

On a recent visit, Oral shared the revelation that was the pivotal point of his life. That moment would change not only him but ultimately also the world! He had received a miraculous healing in his body when he was a young man. It radically changed his life and resulted in his following the call into the ministry.

He and Evelyn were pastors of a small church when he heard the voice of the Lord say these troubling words: "You are not affecting eternity."

Oral went on to explain, "My ministry was a copy of what everyone else was doing. In spite of being supernaturally healed, I was following the pack—no more, no less."

God challenged Oral to read the Gospels and the Book of Acts every single day...on his knees! The turning point came as he read the story where Jesus told Peter that in a certain place he would catch a certain fish. That fish would have a gold coin in its mouth that would enable His disciples to pay their taxes.

The part that got to Oral was where Jesus said, "Take a hook." God was telling Oral, "Get your hook." At that moment, Oral knew that praying for people as Jesus did—by the laying on of hands—was to be his hook.

How did that moment change his life? Oral Roberts has conducted more than three hundred crusades on six continents, and he has written over one hundred twenty books. He is the founder and chancellor of Oral Roberts University in Tulsa, Oklahoma. He has personally laid hands on over *one and a half million people* all around this country using a ten-thousand-seat tent. Perhaps no other person in history has—or ever will—personally lay hands on that many people. I can't tell you how many times I have been in a restaurant with Oral and someone came up and said, "My mother..." or "Our aunt..." or "My grandfather was healed at one of your meetings."

What put me on notice more than anything else I have heard Oral say in all of the stories he has told me was when God told him that he was not affecting eternity. I left that day awakened to the call of the eternal. I am not content to follow the crowd, and I am no longer satisfied with the acceptable life. I want to affect eternity. What about you?

What does it mean to live your life affecting and being affected by eternity? Is this just some mystical mumbo jumbo that has no connection to the *real* world? What if the concept of legacy as it relates to eternity was shown to have scientific significance? I know putting science and spirituality in the same room is dangerous, but we've already crossed that line. Let's stay there and see what science has found that shows a connection between belief and biology as it relates to eternity.

The Bible says that God has placed "eternity" in our hearts—our minds. Could there be any evidence that we have been *hardwired for God*? (See Ecclesiastes 3:10.)

In the book *Why God Won't Go Away: Brain Science and the Biology of Belief,* three scientists explore the neurological aspects of spiritual experiences and awareness.[1] By injecting subjects with a radioactive tracer that is carried by the bloodstream, it's possible to determine which parts of the brain are more or less active under particular circumstances or in a particular individual.

Using a camera that detects radioactive emissions, the scientists photographed the place in the mind that comprehends and connects with the infinite. From praying nuns to people praying in the spirit, pictures of their brains at the peak time of spiritual connection show that prayer stimulates activity in a part of the human brain called the orientation association area (OAA). They call it this, for operational purposes, because the OAA orients a person in physical space. To perform this crucial function, it must first generate a clear, consistent cognition of the physical limits of the self.[2]

In simple terms, the brain must draw a sharp distinction between the individual and everything else to sort out the you from the infinite not you that makes up the rest of the universe. In other words, the spiritual connection is not made up in the imagination. The brain has a place and function designed to recognize and respond to the spiritual.[3]

We are capable of tapping into the infinite—the eternal. God has us hardwired to be able to have knowledge of Him and His ways. This means that we have a biological capacity for experiencing God— eternal things—in ways that can be captured on film. The eternity that God placed in our heart is scientifically detectable. I like to call it our "God space."

Could this be what Christ was describing as the "place" He was preparing for us? "I go to prepare a place for you...that where I am, there you may be also....If anyone loves Me...We [Father and Jesus] will come to him and make *Our home with him*" (John 14:2–3, 23, emphasis added).

Could this hope that Jesus gave the troubled disciples be more than just our heart's home in heaven, but heaven's home in our hearts?

Yes, I believe so. There is a God-given instinct to seek Him, with clues along the path that He intends for us to find and follow.

> "Eye has not seen, nor ear heard, nor have entered into the heart of man the things which God has prepared for those who love Him." But God has revealed them to us through His Spirit.
> —1 Corinthians 2:9–10

It is God who has initiated the hunger and hope in us for Himself and made a place "that where He is we can be also."

Only in the light of eternity will our lives make complete sense. A legacy is our purpose for living between here and eternity.

If science has found a way to identify this "God space" in some shape or form—what a sign! We are indeed capable of connecting to another world—God's world. In that world, our lives connect with a meaning *bigger* than ourselves and *beyond* the here and now.

I'm not one who is looking for my faith to be validated by science. Scripture is quite clear that the way of the God chasers is paved with just enough obstacles for the intellect to trip on, leaving the path only for those who will go beyond human reasoning and trust their intuition (your inner tutor) to the Spirit.

> But the natural man does not receive the things of the Spirit of God, for they are foolishness to him; nor can he know them, because they are spiritually discerned...but we have the mind of Christ.
> —1 Corinthians 2:14, 16

Still, I like knowing that some aspects of my faith can be substantiated by scientific fact. "For since the creation of the world His invisible attributes are clearly seen, being understood by the things that are made, even His eternal power and Godhead, so that they are without excuse" (Rom. 1:20).

It is similar to my love for my wife. Science can explain why I am drawn to the opposite sex. They can demonstrate that there is a certain chemical reaction in my brain that makes falling in love a natural phenomenon. But you could never pinpoint my love for Jeannie with a microscope or an MRI. At some point, science stands outside of the hard facts and data and observes a power of love that defies all reason and theories.

So it is with faith. As Albert Einstein said, "Science without religion is lame. Religion without science is blind."

I want you to comprehend how much thought God has put into your lineage, your life, and your legacy. Let the eternal connection capture your heart. Then allow yourself to realize how every action and attitude is connected to the generations that are *flowing* in your bloodline. Now with one hand holding to the eternal and the other hand grasping the generational, you now are living your personal life in the perfect state of balance. This is where God wants you to live—this is how you live between "here and eternity."

ETERNITY BEGINS NOW

Eternity is not just a *quantity* of life—it's a *quality* of life that we can begin living at the moment of conversion. It's where we came from . . . it's where we are going . . . it's where we can live life right now.

A little boy slipped inside his newborn sister's bedroom. Seeing her son go into the room, the mother eased up to the door and listened to him whisper, "Tell me about God, sis. I've almost forgotten!"

We have all come from the eternal. We will all return to the eternal (be it light or darkness). We are fully alive when we live connected to the eternal—now!

So what does eternity mean to you?

Eternity to you might be the time it takes to stand in line at the grocery store or the amount of time it takes you to get your tax refund.

Oh yeah, you might be thinking that eternity stuff is important, but you're in the middle of a hectic life right now; some other time, please!

We have been given futile minds subject to the superficial. (See

Romans 8:20.) As a result, it's so easy to become trapped by the now and the temporary, deeply imprisoned inside the dungeon of denial of a higher life, the later life of eternity.

Have you found a way to ignore that eternal nudge? Have you convinced yourself that you don't want to live forever anyway and that your longing for the eternal is delusional? Have you silenced what God placed in your heart and dodged the piercing ponderings of eternity?

Eternity is not something imagined by our ego. Eternity is not some egotistical fantasy that we have imagined to pacify our own insecurities.

It is a God-driven instinct that is placed deep within our very being. You want to live forever because you *can* and *will* live forever. It is only this earth suit called your body that fights and feuds with your faith.

No matter how successful you appear to be, with money and recognition and all other measures of our temporary view of success, you will never have a sense of value until you can connect the dots from here and now to the eternal.

Eternity is not only your destination; it's also your guide. Eternity is not just where you are going; it's what gives you the strength to get there. In other words, it's not just a place; it's a perspective. Eternity is a gift that we receive when we believe, and it becomes our guide as we are led by its voice. The voice of the eternal speaks of values and virtues that transcend time and our temporary space here on Earth. Eternity speaks of the bigger, ongoing purpose and plan not seen through the lens of the temporal.

As you surrender to that plan of God, the plan itself surrenders the strength needed to fulfill it.

LIVING IN THE ZONE

Christ lived His life in the power and perspective of "yesterday, today, and forever." He saw His life from a three-dimensional view of time. As a result, He could see into people's pasts, detect their current problems, and speak to their futures, all in the present. He lived in "the zone." He overcame persecutions, endured sufferings, and was never tainted by popularity and power.

In a sense, that's what we can do also; we can live—through Christ—

our lives with wisdom of the past, present, and future simultaneously available to us.

Can you imagine how valuable it is to be able to sense past history, present circumstances, and potential possibilities of the future as you make decisions in your life?

Whoa! You might be thinking, "This guy is out there in the twilight zone." But this premise is just a new twist on the influence of an eternal perspective in our lives. God wants us to be influenced beyond what we can see with our natural eyes. Wisdom is essentially a process of sensing and following an instinct that is beyond us, something supernatural.

I'll make it practical. Let's say you are choosing between two jobs. You don't know which job is the will of God. They both have equal but different opportunities. You are in a dilemma. What if you could go back and see the past of both companies and have a sense of where and how they arrived at where they are now? What if you could fast-forward and see where they will be going in the future? What if you could really know what's behind the promises they are making to you? Are they legitimate?

> **I judge all things only by the price they shall gain in eternity.**
> —**John Wesley**

You pray. While you are praying your spirit discerns something that you can't put your finger (logic) on, but something is just not right with one of the offers you have. Could you be seeing the past, present, and future?

Could eternity be revealing to you what it sees?

Some call it a "gut instinct."

I'm calling it your "God intuition"!

That's all I am saying. Discernment is eternity's evaluation influencing the future of your life...in the present!

It's your **D**ivine **N**avigating **A**ctivation at work.

Legacy helps us live in "the zone." We live with a perspective of our past heritage. Our imaGENEation shows us that in every deed there is a seed. Our present is lived by celebrating a life that is validated by both the past and future. That's getting into the zone—the legacy zone.

Don't live your life without being able to see through the eternal lens of legacy.

It is like the U2 song "Stuck in a Moment You Can't Get Out Of." Are you stuck in the moment? What motivation do you need to get unstuck? What do you need to do to recapture the connection to the eternal that will enlighten your every moment with a clearer sense of meaning?

The restlessness you feel may not be a need to change careers or to buy a new house or to upgrade your external conditions. It may be that you have unplugged from the signals of eternity that were meant to guide and bring meaning to your everyday life. Eternity does not need to compete for its place in our hectic schedules—it can actually complete them, like a backdrop on the stage of our lives, adding just the right setting to allow us to perform to our greatest potential.

Properly responding to the grumpy teller at the bank, being patient with your children, holding back your temper at the grocery line—if eternity is real and legacy is what we do between here and eternity, then everything matters. It all counts for something.

Eternity is not some surreal mystic belief that hovers over your life like a cloud. It's in the magical moment of sowing an action that may reap benefits in the eternal, like teaching a child a holy truth or sharing family stories with the next generation. Every moment that you tune out the noise of the world and tune into what is holy is a moment that touches eternity.

We must eternalize our life in the here and now. What is not eternal is eternally useless. I plead with you to recognize that even now God is bidding you to hear the call of eternity. It is not by chance this book is in your hand. Let it amplify the sound of eternity in your heart.

ETERNALIZE YOUR VISION

It's time for you to step into what God has already determined for you. The time has come for you to live your life with eternity resonating in your every heartbeat. Viewing your life with an eternal perspective will prepare you for that day...*the* day: "He [God] has appointed a day" on which you and I will be judged by "the Man" (Acts 17:31).

You could easily limit your life's purpose by seeing everything only from an *internal* view—forming purpose from your opinions, feelings, and subjective objectives. External pressure could cause you to bow to materialism and to living just for the moment. But a legacy will lift your view to see the *eternal*.

Through the eyes of legacy you can *eternalize* everything that happens to you and through you and gain the perspective to see all things working for you.

Eternal eyes pierce through the shallow and superficial. We see the end; we develop subconscious awareness that we will give account for our lives—that everything *does* matter.

How will you be prepared for that one-on-one, face-to-face conversation with God about your life? Legacy living will help you be right on that day.

Legacy will sow a dream into your heart. Let that dream seduce you to a life that sweeps you off your feet. Live with illogical hope

Eternity matters!

and improbable faith. Embrace your dream. Engage your dream. Experience your dream. The dream is not finished with you yet. The dream will become you.

A real God dream is too meaningful to be understood in your lifetime, too vital to be done alone. Its virtues will live forever.

This vision of the eternal closes the gap between humanity and divinity. This link connects our past, the problems, and the too-often-grueling process to God's determined plan. Eternal eyes will see you through.

CHAPTER 13

Anatomy of a Dream

Legacy—what dreams become

Then they said to one another, "Look, this dreamer is coming!"

—GENESIS 37:19

A LEGACY BEGINS AS A DREAM OF WHAT YOUR FUTURE COULD LOOK like. A dream becomes the seed that blooms in God's garden of generations. Understanding and grasping the dynamics that make up a dream will actually empower you to fulfill the dream.

Dreams are a part of the GPS that comes standard in all humans. Dreams reveal the clues to the destiny that God has for you.

I like the Hebrew word for dream, *chalom*. It means "to make plump, to swell, to extend to its fullness...to enlarge, to make fat." It gives an image of a future that will have you "bursting at the dreams"!

You must never lose the thrill of dreaming. Dreaming is an often-overlooked sign that you are filled with the Holy Spirit. (See Acts 2; Joel 2.) When we lose the pounding of a dream in our chest, we are losing not only that dream but also the legacy that the dream will become.

So what if you have lost the desire to dream? What if you have had one too many disappointments?

You can and you will dream again.

You must know what makes up a dream. One day I thought, "What if you could take a dream apart?" Let's say you were to dissect a dream.

I think you would find three elements, for lack of a better word, that define and describe what a dream is made up of.

The Anatomy of a Dream

Here is what I believe to be the anatomy of a dream:

Hope

All dreams begin with hope—hope for something better, hope that things can be better, hope that you can be better, hope that a brighter day is coming and that you are part of what will make that happen. Hope insists that it can see the invisible. It has the stubborn capacity to believe the impossible and expect the intangible.

Alexander Pope said, "Hope springs eternal."[1]

Never lose hope.

Someone once said, "*Hopeless* is the most profane word you can use. It's like slamming the door in God's face."

Where does hope come from? It is that God deposit I mentioned earlier that is intended to draw us into a desire for better possibilities for our tomorrows. It is the hope that God Himself has placed in us—the "hope to grope"—so that we would seek Him and find Him (Acts 17:27; Rom. 8:20–25).

> **Without hope, the future is nothing more than yesterday dressed up like today and acting like tomorrow.**

We must never let go of the rope of hope that God has placed in our hearts. In Hebrews 6:19, hope is called "the anchor of the soul." Once we've thrown that anchor, we will feel a surge of emotional strength that our human reasoning cannot comprehend or explain. Once we drop anchor and secure our position, we can cast our net into the improbable to capture the impossible.

A boy was standing at the foot of the escalator at a large department store, intently watching the handrail. An employee who was passing by thought the little boy was scared and lost and asked if he needed help. Without taking his eyes off the handrail he replied, "Nope. I'm just waiting for my chewing gum to come back." That's hope. Don't ever lose hope.

What if you are so bogged down in the pain of the past that you can't even hope any longer? Then pray for hope.

"In hope against hope he [Abraham] believed" (Rom. 4:18, NASU). What does that mean?

Sometimes all you can do is just hope! You can get to a place where all you can hope for is hope itself. If your life has become so overwhelmed that the rope to hope has been cut off, pray, like Abraham, that God will give you the hope to hope—again.

If the dates on your calendar change but nothing else changes— hope. If life has become a dreadful repeat performance of the same old drudge and grudge, let me encourage you to let a spark of hope ignite in your heart. Hope will not disappoint.

It may feel like a last-ditch effort. Cast your anchor one more time into the ocean of opportunities. Give hope a chance to latch onto a rock that will secure a place for you to once again dream.

Faith

Hope begins the process and secures our position on the sea of dreams. But hope alone is not enough. There is a second force called *faith*, which can be distinguished from hope. Faith not only *anticipates* what could be, but it also draws us into *action* to make it so. Faith will cast out the net. Faith engages us to take ownership of what we desire. Faith writes up a contract and insists that we sign it. Faith is hope in overalls and with tools in its pocket.

> Now faith is the substance of things hoped for, the evidence of things not seen.
>
> —HEBREWS 11:1

We live by one of two choices—fear or faith! The choice is made in daily, sometimes moment-to-moment decisions.

When one is under the influence of faith, the line that separates imagination from reality disappears. The reality gap is merely a small detail that will be closed by the results of faith; it's just a matter of time. Faith is not bothered by the *facts* of why it can't be done; truthfully, it is quite bored by what we call our reality. The "not yet seen" is where our faith resides and rejoices.

Faith calls that which is not as though it is! Actually, once everyone begins to see the results, faith slips out the back door and moves to another domicile.

> Only that which cannot be seen is of faith.
>
> —2 Corinthians 5:12

Love

Love is the driving force behind all godly dreams. When love is not fueling your dreams, you have nothing more than ambiguous ambition, power without purpose, and deceitful desires. Without love, hope and faith become slaves of precipitous passions that manipulate emotions for self-serving excess that has little resemblance of a true dream's success.

There is a tragic misuse of the power of hope and faith when love is not present. You can have faith that can move mountains, but if you do not have love, it is nothing (1 Cor. 13).

Love is at the very heart of a dream. It is God's love that moves us to dream. The dream begins as a seed planted by God to bear precious fruit.

> **Faith goes up the stairs love built and looks out the window which hope has opened.**[2]
>
> —Charles Spurgeon

Love explains the sacrificial behavior of those in the quest of a dream from God. Love is the justification for the rejection and resistance that a dream will inevitably endure. It is love that will bear and believe all things.

> Love suffers long and is kind; love does not envy; love does not parade itself, is not puffed up; does not behave rudely, does not seek its own, is not provoked, thinks no evil; does not rejoice in iniquity, but rejoices in the truth; bears all things, believes all things,

hopes all things, endures all things. Love never fails. . . . And now abide *faith, hope, love, these three*; but the greatest of these is love.
—1 Corinthians 13:4–8, 13, emphasis added

Where there is no love, a dream will never see the dawning of a legacy. What would seem to be a legacy, without love, will be nothing more than a well-oiled machine of wills and wealth distribution without heart and soul. The legacy might be legal, but it is not lethal. It will not survive the test of time.

Love will hold your legacy together when the scavengers of greed and control attempt to devour it. Love will keep all egos in check.

Without love you have a vision filled with vices.

Through love your dreams will never fail.

Love will rejoice in the victories of your tomorrows—today. It will make sweet the sorrows of your past—today.

WHAT DREAMS BECOME

In all of American history, there is probably no better example of a man with a clear and pure dream than that of the Reverend Dr. Martin Luther King Jr. His dream was so clear, so profound, so simple, and so pure that it took root in thousands of other men and women around the country. Men and women from all creeds and classes, from all races and religions, laid down their differences for one day to march together.

You've seen the grainy black and white footage. The imagery is chilling and beautiful—thousands of men and women arm in arm with a single-minded purpose and bound together by a single dream.

On August 28, 1963, King mounted the steps of the Capitol in his black suit and slim black tie and delivered one of the most memorable speeches in American history, "I Have a Dream." With that speech, Martin Luther King Jr. seized his place in history and perpetuated his legacy.

How about you? Is your life having any effect on eternity? What will you do today that will have any meaning one hundred years from now?

Celebrate your victories. Contemplate your virtues. Collaborate your values. Leave a *bread trail* for your children to follow down the paths that you have walked. Don't let your seed go begging for bread—not just to eat but also to lead them down the paths you have experienced.

The *Magic* of the Disney Legacy

If you've ever been to Disneyland or Disney World, you've seen one of the greatest secular legacies of all time. Walt Disney saw many of his visions come to fruition and achieved huge success in his lifetime. More than that, his name and his legacy are permanently linked with providing exciting and educational experiences for families. How did Walt Disney establish such a legacy?

An idea—vision

It all begins with a vision.

"The voyage that ended with the opening of Disneyland in 1955 really began when Walt was entertaining his little girls on Sundays in the early 1940s. As the children took their fifteenth ride around the merry-go-round, Walt would sit quietly on a wooden bench, wondering why no one had invented a clean, safe place where parents and children could enjoy themselves at the same time."[3]

How many times have you thought of a way to improve the world while sitting on a park bench or driving on the freeway or taking a shower? Whom would you really like to help—children, the poor, or those who do not know Jesus? What would you like to be a part of in your lifetime that would be remembered past your lifetime? Have you ever sensed that you might have an idea, a vision that could change the world?

Research and preparation

Dreaming about how to change the world while sitting on a park bench is only the first step. The next step is to get into action.

What exactly do you want to accomplish? What would it take? Has anyone done it before or done something similar? What can you learn from that person's experiences? Is someone doing it now? Can you team up with that person? What do you need to know to get started?

Walt worked on his vision for years before it became a reality. His research and preparation convinced him that he was on the right path, and that increased his excitement about the possibilities for the vision in his head.

According to the biography, "The idea of his amusement park consumed him. Walt played with a sequence of ideas that grew steadily bigger. He visited amusement parks around the United States and the world. Mostly, he found them to be awful, smelly, dirty, and not particularly safe."[4]

As you think about your vision each day, if it is right, it will continuously be confirmed by what you see and hear. Pay attention.

Perseverance

The idea and vision of Disneyland consumed Walt. His perseverance lit passion in everyone Walt came into contact with. So contagious was the excitement that on opening day it was televised on a ninety-minute live television program, which was the most-watched TV event up to that time.[5]

The success of Disneyland paved the way for Disney World. Walt died before its grand opening. Someone remarked to his wife during the ceremony, "If only Walt could have lived to see the day!"

His wife responded, "He did!" Walt Disney saw the end of what he had envisioned a generation before others did.

As wonderful *as the happiest place on earth* is, it pales in comparison to the real *kingdom*!

THE ETERNAL KINGDOM

A spiritual legacy follows the same basic pattern as Walt Disney's secular legacy. Someone must capture the idea or vision, research the price and cost of that vision, and then persevere against all odds.

A story of a dear family in our church captures the true spirit of the launching of a legacy.

In 1947 Reverend Paul and Pricilla Johnson moved as newlyweds from Minnesota to Siam (now Thailand) to begin living out a vision God had placed on their lives. For five years, they learned the language and traveled by oxcart to various northeastern villages holding meetings and discipleship classes. They were not afraid to be innovative, and as a result, they started the first radio broadcast of the gospel to all of Thailand.

During the last month before their return to the United States for their first furlough, they were holding a gospel meeting in the Hueysampad village, just across the path from where they were staying with their three children. Pricilla was behind the pump organ and Reverend Paul was leading singing in the front of the church. Tragedy struck.

Eight bandits walked into the meeting and began shooting. Pricilla was shot three times, and Reverend Paul was shot five times in the stomach. In desperation to reach her children, Pricilla desperately crawled on her bloody hands and knees out of the meeting room. She would not make it. She died in a nearby banana field. The bandits then went across to where the children were staying and searched for money. They found nothing and fled the village.

Paul was taken to Bangkok by emergency airlift. After days of numerous attempts to sustain his life failed, he passed away. His last words were not words of anger or of questioning God. Paul's last words were, "Father, forgive them."

The end? Not quite.

For years Michael Thomforde's ministry constantly led him to work with missionaries in the field. It did not matter what role he was in—children's ministry, youth ministry, or administration—missions were always dear to his heart. Secretly, he always prayed, "Lord, why couldn't I have been born overseas in a missionary family or had missionaries in my family?" He never said this to anyone.

After many years, his sister was doing some research on the family tree and discovered that he did indeed have a missionary lineage. Reverend Paul and Pricilla Johnson were Michael's great-uncle and aunt!

Michael's call now became clear. A legacy had lured him into the ministry, and it would not stop driving him until he found it. His destiny was in his DNA.

Fifty years after Reverend Paul and Pricilla died, Michael flew to the remote region of their mission and found their gravestones. He knelt down and, with eyes filled with tears, thanked the Lord that they had given their lives for the cause of the good news of Christ. That day he committed to pick up the torch for his family and continue the work.

He and his wife, Gwen, began a mission outreach in the *same* village! Serving Our World, a ministry that rescues children from abandonment and sex trafficking, is now up and running and has become a vital part of the solution to this horrific problem.[6]

Today, just a few years later, God's favor and faithfulness have provided fifteen acres and a Good Life Home and Community Center where God's love is shown in action through meals, education, and daily care for hurting boys and girls.

The entire Thomforde family is involved and working together.

Their son and his wife, Josh and Tayla, have worked in the very same village where Paul and Pricilla gave their lives. They help administer the home and continue the legacy. After applying multiple times to various mission organizations, in the final hours before their departure, would you care to guess which agency granted them their missionary visas? The very same organization that granted visas to Michael's great-uncle and aunt fifty years earlier.

A vision, preparation, and perseverance became the ingredients for the Thomforde's legacy. It may not be as well known as Disneyland here on Earth, but I'm certain Serving Our World is known in heaven, and in eternity it will have more meaning.

- What about your legacy?

- What is the vision of your heart?

- What preparation and research are you engaged in?

- Where is your perseverance expressed?

Today, grant yourself permission to envision what could be. Don't worry about whether you can accomplish the task. Just take the first step as you begin to see the vision.

We are the instruments, not instigators, of the plans of God. Because of that, we shouldn't take our defeats so personally. Don't be dismayed with the battles you may be engaged in right now. The battle is the Lord's—and that of your legacy! You will be victorious. God's plan cannot be denied. The grace of God always brings redemption and rejoicing out of our ruins. We may experience delay in the plans of God by our own actions or by the circumstances beyond our control, but His plans cannot be denied.

Cherish every step of your journey. Contemplate your setbacks as material for increasing your wisdom. Even your disappointments, when shared, can bring much good to others and to the generations who will hear and learn.

You have come to the most phenomenal moment of your life. You now have a sense that everything about you matters. There is no down time, no wasted time, no meaningless moments of wandering through life without a clue. You now know that your life has been strategically set up for a purpose that will impact generations.

Everything—every trial, test, and triumph—is not just personal but generational and has eternal responsibilities and rewards. Your destiny is in your DNA, and the choices you make today will affect your seed tomorrow.

All you need to do is release your faith and faithfulness to the principles of legacy. You don't even need to understand everything.

Like a farmer, just plant the seed and trust the seed to figure out how it will grow. The power of your seed will overcome every obstacle and will find a way to bring forth its fruit. Even if the "birds" of the enemy have found a way to pluck your seed and devour it, do not worry—the seed will not lose its potent power. It will work its way through their system and find good ground and grow. The seed cannot be denied.

Live your life with the understanding that the deeds you sow will become the seeds that will grow for your legacy tomorrow.

THE SPIRITUAL TIPPING POINT

Today is the day to set a new standard. Raise the bar, whether it is high or low. Choose to use the gifts God gave you to become the strongest link in your lineage. The tipping point—the point of turnaround and new beginnings—has come your way.

What is a spiritual *tipping point*? It is a mysterious moment when with minimum movement a miraculous momentum is set in motion.

It's always something little that tips the scales. Sometimes just one little adjustment, one difficult decision, one more act of obedience, one last act of kindness, or one more prayer shakes the heavens and impacts your destiny in a huge way.

In the Bible there are two different Greek words for time. One word, *kronos*, is time as we know it—seconds, minutes, hours, dates on a calendar. The other word, *kairos*, is mentioned eighty-six times. It means "the right or opportune moment, a passing instant when an opening appears, which must be driven through with force, a time of favor, a moment of spiritual opportunity."

Suddenly, what was not valuable is valuable. What nobody wanted—an idea, a company, or a piece of land—everybody now wants. Suddenly, everybody wants to hear your music. Suddenly, everybody wants to buy your product. Suddenly, everybody wants to work with your company.

Suddenly everybody wants to listen to you—your family, friends, and co-workers. It will be clear that something has happened. All you need to do is let this newfound grace do its thing.

Here's the key: prayers never die—they accumulate. You may be one prayer away from a tipping point.

What happened to Cornelius in Acts 10 will happen to you. Cornelius prayed and gave, gave and prayed, and then suddenly the heavens opened. His prayers

You do the right thing over and over, and then do the right thing one more time, and dramatically, something spectacular happens.

and giving had been accumulating as a memorial unto God. That's the tipping point. The Lord rarely moves quickly, but He does move suddenly. God then made some radical moves in order to answer Cornelius's prayers. It wasn't easy. He had to debate with Peter regarding crossing religious lines. He even had to interrupt Peter's sermon so that nothing would be said or done that would hinder the tipping (falling) of the Holy Spirit on the first Gentiles of the Christian faith.

Don't become disheartened and say, "I've cried out to God, and He has not heard me." You are moving God with your prayers and acts of obedience. Nothing wasted. Everything counting. Accumulation.

Don't worry about time, either. God can do in one moment what would be absolutely impossible or take many years of effort on your part. In one second God can restore your family, restore your fortune, heal your marriage, deliver your helpmate, open your womb, or convert a selfish heart to one of service.

One touch of God can remove everything standing in the way of your victory. You can go from being a dead man to having the burial stone rolled away and resurrecting into a new life and having opportunity open before your very eyes—in one divine moment.

GOD'S SUPER BOWL

I love the imagery of the Book of Revelation. It bursts forth from the pages. We need to get over our intimidation of this magnificent book and let the poetic portrait of Christ expand through our imaginations. One of the many incredible images is of the "bowls" of God. (See Revelation 5:8; 16:1; 17:1; 21:9.) This image shows us how prayer is received and responded to—from the earth to heaven and heaven back to the earth. It's about accumulation. Accumulation is a huge asset in the economy of legacy. Everything adds up. Everything counts.

Here is what I think the Scriptures are showing us. The *bowls* hold the prayers of the saints that come from the earth to heaven. The *angels* with *censers* (a cup with an attached long extension for stretching over the altar) transfers the *prayers* with *fire* (to purify). The *incense* (the mix of accumulated prayers of you, others, and Christ) from the *altar* goes before the *throne* of God and then, at the right *kairos* moment, are *thrown* back to the earth in the forms of *voices*, *thunders*, and *lightning* (poetic terms for God's power [Ps. 77:18])! (See Revelation 5:8; 8:3–5; 11:15–19.)

Did you follow that? Read the scriptures, and then read through the previous paragraph again. It's such an encouraging vision to capture in your mind. It will make your every prayer so much more valuable. Prayers start and sustain legacies. If you can pray, you can build an unbelievable legacy.

Every prayer is accumulated throughout all generations. I personally believe we each have a bowl—as does every family lineage, every nation, and even every church. Those bowls become filled with our prayers. The prayers need to be purified; our prayers are often tainted with distorted and destructive motives. Those prayers are continually at work before the throne of God in heaven.

A prayer never dies.

Neither does any other act of faith toward God—giving, fasting, and our good works. At some point in time, a spiritual *tipping point* is reached. When that happens we feel the effect in dramatic ways that can only be described by the images of thunder, lightning, and voices, all of which represent how God is at work on the earth.

There is judgment. Before God can bless, He must on occasion straighten out our messes. (God can't bless our mess!)

There is shaking. God must move obstacles and prepare the way for the answers to your prayers.

In that *kairos* moment everything changes! Salvation comes. Opportunities open. Favor is released.

Miracles are *thrown* back to the earth, and what would normally take years takes mere moments. This is what I call God's Super Bowl!

Nothing you do is ever wasted; everything you do matters—every unjust act inflicted on you or your seed, every effort you put forth, every tear, trial, test—when mixed in the incense of your prayers (and the prayers of those who have gone before you). It all counts for something.

EVERYTHING MATTERS

Legacy is playing in God's Super Bowl, which is taking place right now.

The message of this book has been to show you how God works through your blood and belief in a penetrating and perpetual way. My prayer is that you are stirred, strengthened, and filled with a sustaining passion to follow the personal, generational, and eternal call of legacy.

Are you willing to break away from the temporal and see through the eyes of the eternal? Will you embrace the lives of generations and link to the determined plan of God that was set for you before the foundations of the world? Will you celebrate your legacy? Will you break out of the pack that is caught up in the superficial short-term mind-set of the *me* generation?

When we are committed to living for generational and eternal values, we find that our personal lives take on a quality that enhances every area of our daily lives.

Have Yourself Committed

Skydiving is a fascinating sport. It's a series of small commitments that are completely meaningless unless you make the big commitment. You can drive to the airfield, put on the goggles, strap on the parachute, tie up the boots, and hop into the plane. But unless you're willing to jump out of the door at ten thousand feet, everything else is pointless.

Throwing on a suit, dusting off the Bible, polishing your shoes, and coming to church are meaningless acts unless you're willing to leap into the arms of God with complete abandon.

The first step is always the most difficult. When you commit to unlocking the vision God has for your life, you are preparing to walk on holy ground. Committing to God's vision means that you must lay aside all the paltry distractions and habits that have tossed you about in the past. You must commit your heart, your mind, your body, and everything you possess to God.

What keeps us from committing? The answer is simple: fear—fear of failure, fear of rejection, fear of getting hurt. Some have *phobophobia*— a fear of fear! When people talk about the fear of commitment, they are really talking about these other fears. Somewhere deep in our psyche is the misguided notion that if we do not try, we cannot fail.

Remember the kid on the playground who would lose a game and say, "I wasn't really trying anyway"? What he was really saying is, "I didn't *really* fail. I wasn't *really* committed to winning." What the kid didn't realize is that the failure to commit is a far greater failure than losing itself.

We are afraid to commit to God because we don't want to lose control of ourselves. We are afraid that if we commit our lives to God, we might have to give up our dreams and ambitions.

In short, we don't trust that God's vision for our lives is as good as our own vision for our lives. Guess what—God's vision for your life far exceeds the vision you have for yourself. The depth of joy you will attain by following God's vision is incalculable. You will get something you cannot even imagine, and you will not even have to sacrifice your personal desires (although your may have to sacrifice your need to control the timing)! God gave you those desires in the first place.

What else are we afraid of? We are afraid that by committing to

God, we will somehow become trapped in a life that we never wanted. The irony is that if we aren't committed to God, we are already trapped in a life we never wanted. The longer we refuse to commit our lives to God, the deeper and tighter our entanglements grow.

There are a million ways to avoid committing. There is only one way to commit. Remember how Pharaoh loaded down the Israelites with hours of extra labor in an effort to distract them from their one true desire? Sometimes we are our own Pharaoh. Because we are afraid to commit our lives to God's vision for us, we distract ourselves with work, with friends, with substances, with entertainment. We anesthetize ourselves with activity. We blind ourselves in a whirlwind of superfluity. Every distraction from our commitment to God is another link in our shackles and another stripe on our back.

The answer is simple. Lay down every desire, habit, vice, and doubt that distracts you from God. Turn away from every dissenting voice, and offer yourself a living sacrifice, holy and acceptable unto Him.

A legacy awaits you. A whole new world bids you to come.

The great thing about skydiving is that once you jump, there is really no question about which way you will be going. The laws of gravity and terminal velocity dictate that when you jump out of an airplane, your body will streak directly toward the earth at exactly 212 miles per hour.

The beautiful thing about committing to God is that once you've done it, you are on a divine trajectory, with the laws of God propelling you.

Are you driving to the airfield yet? Are you putting on the goggles, lacing up the boots, hopping into the plane?

Can you feel the wind against your face? Can you feel the cold metal of the doorway against your fingertips?

Can you hear God saying, "Jump! Jump! I'll catch you"?

Well...what are you waiting for? *Jump!*

Legacy Confession

- I am a part of the local church with my time, talent, and treasures. Together we are the expressed body of Christ.

- I am committed to covenant relationships. I welcome authority and accountability. I will not let selfish, short-term, superficial attitudes destroy my family and friends.

- I will prosper. It is a healthy sign that I am a part of the kingdom of God. I will create wealth with the power God gave me. I will be a channel of wealth for my God and my seed.

- This is my mandate. This is my ministry. This is my mission. I will serve my generation well.

—Phil Munsey

Notes

Chapter 1
The Generational-Driven Life

1. Richard Llewellyn, *How Green Was My Valley* (New York: Scribner, 1997).

2. Dr. James D. Watson is credited with discovering the structure of DNA in 1953, and with the start of the human genome project. See Nicholas Wade, "Reading the Book of Life: A Historic Quest; Double Landmarks for Watson: Helix and Genome," *New York Times*, June 27, 2000, http://query.nytimes .com/gst/fullpage.html?sec=health&res=940DE5D81230F934A15 755C0A9669C8B63 (accessed August 1, 2007).

3. For purposes of this discussion, I use the terms *DNA*, *genes*, and *blood* interchangeably, much as Scripture uses *seed*, *descendants*, and *nations* interchangeably. I understand that there are significant biological differences, but I am not a doctor or a scientist. My intent is to make a case for the "transferable" ability that is at work in our natural bodies through the blood.

4. Rick Warren, *The Purpose-Driven Life* (Grand Rapids, MI: Zondervan, 2002).

5. Joel Osteen, *Your Best Life Now* (New York: FaithWords Publishing, 2004).

CHAPTER 2
BIOLOGY OF BELIEF

1. For more information about Tom Riles and "Save 3 Lives Today," go to www.save3livestoday.com.

2. Malta National Blood Transfusion Service, "History," http:// www.health.gov.mt/nbts/history.htm (accessed September 18, 2007).

3. Britannica.com, "Huitzilopochtli," *Encyclopedia Britannica Online*, http://www.britannica.com/eb/article-9041446/ Huitzilopochtli (accessed August 1, 2007).

4. Amanda Ewart Toland, PhD, "Genetics 101 DNA Mutations," *Genetic Health*, http://www.genetichealth.com/G101_Changes_in_DNA.shtml (accessed August 2, 2007).

5. Paul Tillich, *Dynamics of Faith* (New York: Harper and Row, 1958).

6. Robert Wright, "The TIME 100: James Watson & Francis Crick," *TIME*, http://www.time.com/time/time100/scientist/profile/watsoncrick.html (accessed August 2, 2007).

7. Matt Ridley, *Genome: The Autobiography of a Species in 23 Chapters* (New York: Harper Perennial, 2006), 6.

8. Again, throughout the book we will use *DNA*, *genes*, and *blood* as interchanging terms.

9. Dean Hamer, *The God Gene* (New York: Doubleday, 2005).

10. University of Minnesota, "The Minnesota Twin Family Study," http://www.psych.umn.edu/psylabs/mtfs/ (accessed August 2, 2007).

Chapter 3
What You Believe You Leave

1. U.S. Securities and Exchange Commission, "Oldest Baby Boomers Turn 60!" http://www.sec.gov/news/press/extra/seniors/agingboomers.htm (accessed September 18, 2007).

2. Cortland.edu, "Erik Erikson's 8 Stages of Psychosocial Development: Stage 7, Middle Adulthood," http://web.cortland.edu/andersmd/ERIK/stage7.HTML (accessed August 2, 2007).

3. Lou Holtz, *Wins, Losses, and Lessons* (New York: HarperCollins, 2006).

Chapter 6
Generation Against Generation

1. Michael Roberts, *The Faber Book of Modern Verse* (London: Faber and Faber, 1936).

2. Paul Pearsall, *The Heart's Code* (New York: Broadway Books, 1999).

3. Frederick Elmer Bolton, *Principles of Education* (New York: Charles Scribner's Sons, 1910), 193–194.

4. Ibid., 194–195.

5. Dr. James Kennedy and Jerry Newcombe, *Lord of All* (Coral Ridge Presbyterian Church, 2006).

CHAPTER 7
SPOT REMOVAL FOR GENES

1. Ralph Blumenthal, "A 12th Dallas Convict Is Exonerated by DNA," *The New York Times*, January 18, 2007, http://select .nytimes.com/gst/abstract.html?res=F40D13F93A540C7B8DDD A80894DF404482 (accessed September 13, 2007).

2. About.com, "DNA Exonerates 200th Innocent Convict," April 24, 2007, http://crime.about.com/b/a/257393.htm (accessed August 6, 2007).

3. Sherman A. Minton, *Venomous Reptiles* (Basingstoke, Hampshire: Macmillan Publishing, 1982).

4. Eugene H. Peterson, *Reversed Thunder* (New York: HarperOne, 1991), 130.

5. For more information about Birth Choice Health Clinics, see www.birthchoiceclinic.org/ (accessed August 9, 2007).

CHAPTER 8
BONDING OR BONDAGE?

1. Hamer, *The God Gene*.

2. Rabbi Yaakov Kleiman, "Jewish Genes," Judaism Online, http://www.simpletoremember.com/vitals/jewish-genetics.htm (accessed August 9, 2007).

3. Dr. Wes Stafford, *Too Small to Ignore* (Colorado Springs, CO: WaterBrook Press, 2007).

4. Graemme Marshall, "The Olympic Ideal," *Virtual Christian Magazine*, http://vcmagazine.org/vcm/article.asp?volume=2&issue=8&article=olympic (accessed August 9, 2007).

5. Ibid.

CHAPTER 9
MARRIAGE: WHY KNOT?

1. Pew Research Center, "Are We Happy Yet?" February 13, 2006, http://pewresearch.org/pubs/301/are-we-happy-yet (accessed September 20, 2007).

2. Adam Bellow, *In Praise of Nepotism: A Natural History* (New York: Doubleday, 2003).

3. Claude Levi-Strauss, "The Family," in *Man, Culture, and Society*, ed. by Harry L. Sharpiro (New York: Oxford University Press, 1971), 341.

4. U.S. Census Bureau, "American Community Survey 2005," http://www.census.gov/acs/www/ (accessed August 9, 2007).

5. Dietrich Bonhoeffer, *Prisoner for God: Letters and Papers From Prison*, Eberhard Bethge, ed. (New York: The Macmillan Company, 1960), 25–32.

6. Derek Prince, *God Is a Matchmaker* (Grand Rapids, MI: Chosen, 1986).

7. For more information about Paul and Toni or their ministry, Acres of Love, e-mail info@acresoflove.org.

CHAPTER 10
BLOOD, SWEAT, AND TEARS

1. Gordon MacDonald, quoted in GenerousGiving.org, "Key Quotations on Generous Giving: God's Ownership and Man's Stewardship," http://www.generousgiving.org/page.asp?sec=80&page=348 (accessed September 17, 2007).

2. Jim Elliott, quoted in Terry Parker, David H. Wills, and Gregory Sperry, "Designing a Family Stewardship Philosophy," http://www.focusonthefamily.com/stewardship/A000000520.cfm (accessed September 17, 2007).

3. Randy Alcorn, *Money, Possessions, and Eternity* (Wheaton, IL: Tyndale, 2003).

4. Ibid., 46.

5. Microsoft.com, "Microsoft Announces Plans for June 2008 Transition for Bill Gates," http://www.microsoft.com/presspass/press/2006/jun06/06-15CorpNewsPR.mspx (accessed August 13, 2007).

6. Carol J. Loomis, *Fortune*, "Warren Buffet Gives Away His Fortune," CNNMoney.com, http://money.cnn.com/2006/06/25/magazines/fortune/charity1.fortune/index.htm (accessed August 13, 2007).

7. Don Hechinger and Daniel Golden, "The Great Giveaway," *Wall Street Journal Online*, July 8, 2006, http://www.cfah.org/news/060710giveaway.pdf (accessed August 13, 2007).

8. Mike Hayes, *God's Law of First Things* (Ventura, CA: Regal Books, 2004).

9. Vassar.edu, Stephen King Commencement Address, May 20, 2001, Vassar College, Poughkeepsie, New York, http://commencement.vassar.edu/2001/010520.king.html (accessed August 14, 2007).

10. Quoted from a personal conversation with Dr. Schuller.

11. For more information about *Outreach to Africa*, see http://www.outreachtoafrica.org/006a.html (accessed August 14, 2007).

CHAPTER 12
FROM HERE TO ETERNITY

1. Andrew Newberg, Eugene D'Aquili, and Vince Rause, *Why God Won't Go Away: Brain Science and the Biology of Belief* (New York: Ballantine Books, 2002).

2. Ibid., 4–9.

3. Ibid.

CHAPTER 13
ANATOMY OF A DREAM

1. Alexander Pope, "Essay on Man," 1.3.2.

2. Charles Spurgeon, http://www.inspirationpeak.com/cgi-bin/search.cgi?search=faith (accessed September 19, 2007).

3. Katherine Greene and Richard Greene, *The Man Behind the Magic: The Story of Walt Disney* (New York: Viking Juvenile, 1998).

4. Ibid.

5. Ibid.

6. For more information about Michael and Gwen Thomforde or Serving Our World Ministries, see www.servingourworld.org/index.htm (accessed August 24, 2007).

Biography of
Phil M. Munsey

PHIL MUNSEY HAS SERVED IN FULL-TIME MINISTRY FOR OVER THIRTY years. He pastors Life Church, a healthy church of more than two thousand members located in Mission Viejo, California, which he and his wife, Jeannie, cofounded in January 1985.

Phil is an influencer among influencers. He serves many ministries in official capacities, including Joel Osteen/Lakewood Church, Tommy Tenney/God Chasers International, John Maxwell/Equip Leadership Associate and Integrity Leadership Ministries, among others.

Phil's love for the Bible, his knowledge of culture, and his positive worldview, mixed with his deep Spirit-filled roots (three generations) makes his ministry style one that stimulates the mind and stirs the spirit. Phil and Jeannie have been married for more than thirty years and currently reside, along with their horse, Shoko, in Orange County, California. Their three grown children—Kara, along with her husband, Doug Bisel; Phillip II; and Andrew—participate in perpetuating the legacy.

Phil Munsey is committed to living by the motto, "You can touch the world if you don't care who gets the credit."